OLD FORGE

A SURVIVOR'S TALE

The true life of a wireless operator/air gunner
From enlistment in 1940 to demobilisation in 1946

World War II

First Edition 2009

Published by
Old Forge Publishing
39 Backgate
Cowbit
Lincolnshire
PE12 6AP
oldforgepub@aol.com
www.oldforgepublishing.co.uk
01406 381313

Designed by
Jupper Peep
www.jupperpeep.com

ISBN 978-1-906183-12-7

Printed for Old Forge Publishing
in Great Britain by the MPG Books Group,
Bodmin and King's Lynn

Contents

Preface .... **XI**

Glossary .... **XII**

Acknowledgements   **XVII**

Chapter 1 .... Enlistment **3**
                                                   Cardington

Chapter 2 .... Pre-Training **8**
                                                   Blackpool
                                                   Cardington
                                                   Swinderby

Chapter 3 .... Training **10**
                No.10 Reception Centre   Blackpool
                No. 1 Signals School   Cranwell
                Practical experience   Benson
                No.9 Bombing and Gunnery School   Penrhos

Chapter 4 .... Operational Training **19**
                No.1 OTU   Silloth

Chapter 5 .... Operations **23**
                206 Squadron   Aldergrove

Chapter 6 .... Aboard HMS *Keppel* **37**
                                                   Londonderry

Chapter 7 .... Operations **40**
                206 Squadron   Benbecula

Chapter 8 .... Failed To Return 61
Chapter 9 .... Non-Ops Flying 64
                CCDU   Dale/Angle
Chapter 10 ..... Aboard HMS *United* 80
                                         Pembroke Dock
Chapter 11 ..... Non-Ops Flying 82
                ASWDU   Thorney Island
Chapter 12 ..... Demobilisation 91
Chapter 13 ..... Postcript 94

Appendices 96
                I Silloth 97
                II Aldergrove 99
                III Benbecula 102
                IV CCDU Angle 105
                V ASWDU Thorney Island 107
                VI Authors tour of duty 108
                VII Airfields visited 110
                VIII Aircraft flown 112
                IX Ranks held and pay structure 114
                X Pilots 116

Preface

The original intention was to produce a book entitled 'The Families' which would cover the histories of our four main families; the Nelsons, the Shefferds, the Larcombes and the Selfs.

I also hoped to cover the past histories of the many associated people who produced the wives and husbands of the four original families.

As I knew that two World Wars had had their impact, there were to be sections set aside for suitable anecdotes, not least relating to the my six years as an Air Gunner in the RAF. There was also my brother in law Colin's time as the 'eyes and ears' of General Montgomery during the Allied advances out of the Normandy beachhead and on into Germany.

Much of the detail I recorded to mind in the middle of the night. Our dear friend Veronica, poetess 'extraordinaire' and prime mover in the Wiltshire 'Moonrakers Writers Club' proposed that I acquire a pocket size tape recorder. My Niece, Onita's husband, Alex, heard of this suggestion and generously provided one within 24 hours.

The facts were to be gleaned from the records I compiled in 1990 and 2000, when studying Genealogy, and from my wartime flying log books.

In the event, I started on my RAF career and became so 'carried away' that this has become a story in itself.So follows a 'Survivor's Tale', from my enlistment in 1940 to demobilisation in 1946, 'The Life of a Wireless Operator/Air Gunner'. By the time you read this, I hope to be well advanced with 'The Families'.

Glossary

AC..Aircraftsman
ACM u/t..Aircraftmen under training
AFC ....Air Force Cross
API ....Air Position Indicator
ARP ....Air Raid Precautions
ASV ....Airborne Surface Vessel
ASWDU ....Air Sea Warfare Development Unit
ATA...Air Transport Auxiliary
BABS ....Beam Approach Beacon System
BAE ....British Aerospace Systems
CCDU ....Coastal Command Development Unit
CLA ....Creeping Line Ahead
CO ....Commanding Officer
Cpl...Corporal
DF... Direction Finder
DFC ....Distinguished Flying Cross
DR ....Dead Reckoning
DSO...Distinguished Service Order
Fg Off ....Flying Officer
Flt Lt ....Flight Lieutenant
Flt Sgt..Flight Sergeant
FTR ....Failed to Return
GC ....Good Conduct
HF ....High Frequency
HMS ....His Majesties Ship

IFF .... Identification Friend or Foe
IOM .... Isle of Man
LAC ....Leading Aircraftsman
MF .... Medium Frequency
MT .... Motor Transport
MV .... Merchant Vessel
NAAFI .... Navy Arm Air Force Force Institute
NCO .... Non Commissioned Officer
OTU .... Operational Training Units
Plt Off .... Pilot Officer
PO .... Petty Officer & Post Office
POW .... Prisoner of War
PRO .... Public Relations Officer
RAE .... Royal Aircraft Establishment
RN .... Royal Navy
RP .... Rocket Projectile
RS .... Radio School
R/T .... Radio Transmitter
SE .... Special Equipment
Sgt .... Sergeant
SNCO .... Senior Non Commissioned Officer
SOS .... Save Our Souls
u/s .... Unservicable
VE .... Victory in Europe
VJ .... Victory in Japan
WAAF .... Womens Auxiliary Air Force
W/O .... Warrant Officer
WO/AG .... Wireless Operator Air Gunner
Wg Cdr .... Wing Commander
W/T .... Wireless Transmitter

Acknowledgements

My warm thanks to John Bell, affectionately known to his many, many friends and customers as 'John the Fish'. It is largely due to his continued pressure over a long period that the possibility of writing a book grew from a belief into a reality. Thank you John.

Huge thanks also go to Veronica for both her constant encouragement and preparation of the book. She gave up countless hours of her time, week in, week out, over the last three months of 2008, editing, correcting and finally typing it all into her computer. She then produced two manuscripts and two discs. Her most arduous task though must have been the production of the many, many tables of statistics, ranging from the Hudson and Fortress losses through to the ranks held and pay structure. There are some debts in life which cannot be repaid. This is one of them.

Massive thanks also to my fabulous wife Ona for listening time and again to each section and offering such valuable criticisms. Without her love, patience and tolerance it would not have been possible.

Old Forge Publishing would like to thank John Lowe for his help in providing Fortress photographs. His website www.coastalcommand206.com dedicated to his grandfather Ken Bass who served with 206 Squadron.

A SURVIVOR'S TALE

Chapter 1

Enlistment

Shortly after my 17th birthday, a school friend approached me in front of my mother's Home Made cake shop at 56 Romsey Road, Shirley, Southampton. He explained that he had just heard about the pay levels in the RAF and informed me that not only could we earn twelve shillings and sixpence, (12/6d) per day (equal to today's 62½ pence or less than £4.50 a week, but also be issued with a revolver.

In the event, we started as Aircraftmen under Training (ACM u/t) at two shillings per day, (10 pence). In Appendix 9 there is a table of all the different rates earned at the various ascending ranks, from which it can be seen that it was not until I was commissioned in July 1943 that I was issued with a Smith and Wesson revolver and received the 12/6d per day that I had been expecting.

The revolver, however, proved more of an encumbrance than an asset, bearing in mind the need for ensuring it's security at all times. It did, however, help to rescue four of us from a tight spot in the Algiers Casbah on the 18th January 1944, but more of that in Chapter 9.

Despite having absolutely no knowledge of aeroplanes, or of the RAF itself, we caught a tramcar at the Shirley terminus and rattled down to the Recruiting Office in Dorset Street. It is now no longer in existence. (The whole area was blown away in the Air Raids).

On giving my full name, I was directed into the Royal Navy section and it was some time before I could escape. They seemed to think that an Edward Horatio Nelson <u>must</u> be a natural sailor.

In the RAF office I lied and I assured them that I really was 18, born in 1922, and needed to become aircrew, whatever that implied. I did not let on that my knowledge of anything that went on in the sky was virtually zero. I had seen airships, presumably the R-100 or R-101, in the skies over London, I had seen the Schneider Trophy Sea planes over Southampton, as they raced above the Solent to Calshot, but nothing else.

FORM 2168

ROYAL AIR FORCE VOLUNTEER RESERVE.

NOTICE PAPER.

DURATION OF THE PRESENT EMERGENCY.

Signature of Man receiving the Notice Paper ....*Edward St. Nelson*..............

NOTICE to be given to a Man at the time of his offering to join The Royal Air Force Volunteer Reserve.

Date..*13 July*.........19*40*

The General Conditions of the Contract of Enlistment that you are about to enter into with the Crown are as follows :—

1. You will engage to serve His Majesty as an airman for the duration of the present Emergency, provided His Majesty should so long require your services.

2. On enlistment into the Royal Air Force Volunteer Reserve, you will be liable, if medically fit, to carry out duty in the air in any type of aircraft and may be ordered to serve in any part of the world, ashore or afloat.

3. Your term of Service shall begin to reckon from the date of Attestation.

4. The age given by you on enlistment will be accepted as your true age, and you will be liable to be held to serve on the engagement for which you attest notwithstanding that at some future date you may prove that your age given on enlistment is incorrect.

5. Men in receipt of a disability pension are not eligible for enlistment.

6. You will be attested by the Attesting Officer. On completion of your attestation you will be subject to all the provisions of the Air Force Act for the time being in force.

7. You will be required by the Attesting Officer to answer the questions printed on pages 2 and 3, to take the oath shown on page 4, and you are warned that if at the time of your attestation you wilfully or knowingly make any false answer to him you will thereby render yourself liable under the Air Force Act to a maximum punishment of two years' imprisonment with hard labour.

8. If, after arrival at the R.A.F. Recruits Centre, you refuse to enlist for personal reasons, you must be prepared to make your own arrangements for your return journey home. No undertaking can be given that a free warrant would be issued to you.

Signature and Rank of the Officer or Non-Commissioned)
Officer serving the Notice

4

With the Notice Paper duly signed on the 13th July 1940, I then waited to be contacted in due course.

The two of us duly returned to Shirley and I was soon enthusiastically telling my mother all about it. The main gist of her reply was;

"We will see what Father has to say"

I protested that I had already committed myself but to no avail.

My father duly came home and, on hearing the news, announced in typical Arthur George Nelson fashion that we were to return to the Recruiting Office at once where he would advise them that I was born in 1923 and therefore only 17 and underage. This was one of the first crises in my life.

The thought of the pending ignominy if we did go back, the prospect of losing 12/6d a day not to mention the revolver were altogether just too much to bear. I calmly announced therefore that if he did go down there and shame me I would run away and never come back. So it was reluctantly agreed that I could proceed with my enlistment.

The original Notice Paper, Form 2168, is still in my possession and will be passed, along with other war time memorabilia, to our dear friend Mike Hughes, the Scottish historian and author, for display in the three museums he is involved with in Oban, Tiree and Benbecula. He will be their custodian, releasing any of them to family members on request.

As well as the original 'Notice' I also still possess the frail slip of paper recording the original Service No.1181644 with which I was issued at Cardington just five days later. I never cease to marvel at the speed with which it all progressed. To be in Dorset Street on the 13th and contacted, issued with travel details and a rail warrant on the 18th. Then to be transported to Bedfordshire, taken by lorry to Cardington itself and mesmerised by the sight of the gigantic hangers which were needed for the airships. It was a virtual wonderland.

There was little chance to become entranced by the sight of the airship hangers and the considerable number of young lads arriving because almost immediately one was being regimented.

The first night in a large barrack room was quite dreadful. Up until then I had led a fairly sheltered life. Most recently within the gentlemanly confines of the King Edward VI Grammar School and as a Patrol Leader in the 6th (Southampton) St Paul's Troop of Boy Scouts.

I was wholly unprepared for the barrage of so-called jokes, quite horrible smutty stories and was greatly relieved when 'Reveille' sounded. Remember, this was 1940, not 2008.

The days that followed included much waiting queuing, as the hundreds of volunteers were assessed. There were intelligence tests galore, a variety of IQ assessments, health tests, repeated and extended, until after nine days, on the 26th July, I was finally accepted as being suitable for Air Crew training, as a Wireless Operator/Air Gunner (WOP/AG).

By this time, the mass of volunteers had reduced to quite a small number. It was really quite a saddening experience to see the many enthusiastic volunteers crowding into Cardington, dispersing on a daily basis until only a handful remained to be considered eligible for aircrew training.

Firstly, those who could not pass all the health tests were either rejected for service or passed onto other centres for consideration as ground staff, with hundreds of options given to them, all of which were essential.

Numbers continued to dwindle as the intelligence tests took their toll and the final segregation took place. Pilots led the field, followed by navigators and then the WOP/AG's.

In all my six years in the RAF, I never once met a pilot who should have been anything else; maybe the odd navigator who could have been a pilot but certainly all the WOP/AG's I knew were correctly categorised by the Selection Boards.

The process was virtually perfect and is doubtless continued to this day. Many a private company could make good use of their expertise. I have never ceased to be grateful to the teaching staff at King Edward's for my education from 1934 to 1939 or to the Management at H. J. Heinz for the training I received in the few months I was there, early in 1940, covering accountancy, supply and distribution as well as the induction of a sense of self confidence which was essential for a Heinz employee.

So on the 27th July, having now been kitted out with our RAF uniforms and kit bag, we received more travel instructions, a rail warrant and rations for the journey to the No.9 Reception Centre at Blackpool for two weeks of basic training. Drilling on the promenades!!

Before closing this chapter on enlistment, I would have preferred the opening to have recounted my sighting of two or three boat loads of French sailors. They were sighted alongside a quay in Southampton New Docks, probably two to three weeks after completion of the Dunkirk evacuation.

I would have liked to have recorded that I was so moved by the sight of the handful of French military survivors having escaped across the Channel that I dashed to a recruiting office and enlisted in the fervency of patriotism. Instead I have to admit that I viewed them more with curiosity than anything else and I cannot recollect any feelings of real concern or indeed of patriotism. To a young ex-schoolboy the reality of war was far away somewhere in another world. It was only the lure of 12/6d per day _and_ a revolver that prompted my entry into the RAF.

The author 'kitted out' in September 1940

Chapter 2
Pre-Training

After the fortnight spent square bashing at Blackpool, the following seven weeks, from the 10th August to the 30th September, were again spent at Cardington, but this time I was on the staff of the Station HQ. This was quite an elevated position compared with my time there two weeks earlier as a very young 'sprog'.

The Battle of Britain was by now well underway and there were real concerns that an invasion was imminent. We were hastily trained in the use of the .303 rifle and assisted in the digging of defensive trenches around the airfield.

Our task was to man the trenches at night and to be prepared to repel any airborne landing by German paratroopers. Being issued with a single clip of five cartridges did little to enhance our morale. In the daytime, we were the ones now looking after the new arrivals when we were not catching up on our sleep!

Finally, on the 30th September, we were moved to an RAF operational airfield at Swinderby, Lincs, by which time I had chummed up with Brian Spence. We still meet up on occasion at the 206 Squadron re-unions and we remained friends right through training and onto operational flying.

On arrival at Swinderby, we were advised that, due to a lack of accommodation, we would need to sleep in canvas bell tents. There were many groans of dismay at this prospect but, remembering the number of times I had encamped in them with the Scouts I asked if there were any fellow Scouts in our small party and there was just one. So the two of us set about indoctrinating the rest into the joys of camping! We were attached to the Signals Section and spent a great deal of time servicing the external field telephone systems.

One day, Brian and I decided that we would endeavour to visit the great Cathedral city of Lincoln. After a long walk from Swinderby airfield to the main road, we attempted to thumb a lift, hitch hiking being fairly prevalent in those early war days.

'Ere long, a chauffeur driven limousine pulled up alongside us and the driver enquired as to where we were heading.

'To Lincoln' we replied and were promptly invited to join the other occupant in the rear of the car. In the half light we slowly made out the features of the passenger and were left speechless as we realised we were in the company of that great actor, David Niven. (The sequel to this is recorded in Chapter 12 which includes comments on the 206 Squadron Association's post war reunions).

Swinderby's operational squadrons were 300 and 301, both Polish. They were flying Fairey Battle's, mainly against the Channel ports. Their losses were many and there was an air of tragedy everywhere.

Finally, as the colder weather crept in, we were despatched to the No.10 Reception Centre at Blackpool for our initial wireless and Morse code training, up to 12 words per minute.

At last, three and a half months after enlisting, we were to be in full training.

Chapter 3
Training (Section 1)

From the 1st November 1940 until the 14th February 1941, a further three and a half months into my RAF career, we moved away from the realities of life on RAF airfields and found ourselves living in Bed and Breakfast accommodation in Lancashire.

Our first 'digs' found us in a terraced property built for half our number. Conditions were far from ideal, cramped bedrooms, poor washing facilities and all of us squashed into a tiny dining area at breakfast and evening meal times. We grumbled, we complained, we envied those in the larger properties, all to no avail. So we literally just soldiered on and looked forward to our return to a proper RAF camp.

Our daytime classroom was huge. I think the main one was part of the Blackpool Tower. Not the main ballroom as that was still available for dancing, here we first of all had to learn the Morse code alphabet.- -... -.-. (A B C and so on). We could not have mastered it very quickly in Class No.1C12 as it was not until five weeks later, on the 9th of December, that we had our first test at 4 words per minute. I passed with an 'A' grade, sending and receiving plain language and coded 4 mixed letter/numeral groups, e.g. W8P6, 3N1Q.

We were also being lectured on wireless telegraphy as well as the make up of various types of operational radios. Additionally, most days included a long session on the promenade, drilling, marching and countermarching and gradually having instilled in us a pride in Class 1c12. We were slowly realising the importance of teamwork and being members of a close knit squad, needing to be smarter than the others. We began marching for each other and for the squad. Class 1c12 became a unit where one's loyalty was to the squad. What an amazing transformation, from the mixed bag of youngsters who had so recently arrived in Blackpool.

The speed of our Morse code progress was measured in weeks; we had to learn the code and then be able to reach 12 words per minute, sending and receiving, within an overall total of 14 weeks. In peacetime, it used to take a full year. So 4 w.p.m. by December 9th

SEMAPHORE SIGNS AND SIGNIFICATIONS

A & 1	B & 2	C & 3	D & 4	E & 5
F & 6	G & 7	H & 8	I & 9	J
K & 0	L	M	N	O
P	Q	R	S	T
U	V	W	X	Y
Z	Alphabetical	Numeral	Annul	

SIGNS USED WITH THE MORSE CODE

SIGNALLING RULES

A *dash* is three times the length of a *dot*. The interval between the component parts of a sign is equal in duration to one dot; that between each complete sign forming a word or group to one dash or three dots; and that between words or groups to two dashes or six dots. A dash over the signs indicate that the letters are made without pausing between them.

1. ALPHABET

Symbol.	Meaning.	Symbol.	Meaning.
· —	A	— ·	N
· — · —	ā or "A barred"	— — · — —	n̄ or "N barred"
— · · ·	B	— — —	O
— · · · —	b̄ or "B barred"	— — — ·	ō or "O barred"
— · — ·	C	· — — ·	P
— · — · —	c̄ or "C barred"	· — — · —	p̄ or "P barred"
— — — —	Ch	— — · —	Q
— · ·	D	· — ·	R
·	E	· · ·	S
· · — · ·	e or "E barred"	—	T
· · — ·	F	· · —	U
— — ·	G	· · — —	ū or "U barred"
· · · ·	H	· · · —	V
· ·	I	· — —	W
· — — —	J	— · · —	X
— · —	K	— · · — ·	x̄ or "X barred"
· — · ·	L	— · — —	Y
— —	M	— — · ·	Z

'A'; 5 w.p.m. by December 16th, another 'A'; 6 w.p.m. by December 23rd, 'A' again; 7 w.p.m. on December 27th, only an 'A-' and so on to until 12 w.p.m. was reached on January 24th, all 'A's'.

My RAF form 1467, containing details of my 12 w.p.m. test, was kept by the instructor. The original forms, covering the 4 w.p.m. to 11 w.p.m. tests, are still in my possession however, yellowing with age.

I now notice that in the 4 w.p.m. test the longest word was only seven letters – 'nations' whereas by the 11 w.p.m. test it had grown to nine – 'screening' and indeed most of the words in the message were much longer than in the earlier ones.

So we had advanced from sending and decoding twenty five letters in 60 seconds to seventy letters in the minute. All in just over six weeks and that included Christmas.

Christmas in Blackpool sounds blissful - not for us in our cramped 'digs'. At lunch on Christmas Day, the landlady dished up plates of greasy goose. The smell was not pleasant, the presentation was awful. In fact, it was so depressing that we all just pushed our chairs back and squeezed out of the room on the verge of tears. We spent the rest of Christmas Day on the promenade, cold, unhappy and each one of us desperately homesick. At 17½, one is not prepared for an event like this on Christmas Day and I am sure we would have liked nothing better than to run away from it all and return home. Our distress must have reached the ears of the billeting officer as, shortly afterwards, we were all moved into a bright, clean, spacious guest house.

8: 12 with paper kept by R.A.F.

R.A.F. Form 1467

ROYAL AIR FORCE.

STANDARD MORSE EXERCISE. I C 12

Test _11 (eleven)_ W.P.M.   Date _24 Jan 1941_   Class _I.C.12_

Name _NELSON. E.H_   Number _1181644_   Rank _Ac2_

Receiving Results.		Corrector's Signature.	Assessment and Remarks.		Signal Officer's Signature.
Part	Mistakes				
1			Receiving		
2			Sending		
3			Procedure		
TOTAL			Visual		

PART I.—PLAIN LANGUAGE.

The	aerial	must be	erected	clear
of	any	metal	object	thus
reducing	screening	effect		
		'SYKO'		
S31H	F24Q	6D0M	AL59	KP6B
YT8J	2i4R	P8C7	1PQ3	509E
				T of O

PART II.—LETTER GROUPS ⎱ overleaf.
PART III.—FIGURE GROUPS ⎰

Wt. 8319/5145   90,000 Pads   5/40   W. H. & S.   658/34

At some time during our spell in Blackpool, there were severe air raids on the South Coast Ports and London. Leave passes and travel warrants were issued to anyone living in or north of London, each with a maximum duration of 48 hours. I was not eligible as it was not deemed possible for anyone to travel to and return from a destination south of London within that limited period.

I had heard nothing from my parents or sisters and, feeling certain that one of the South Coast Ports was 'Southampton', I decided to travel home. I had no money of any significance so I would need to rely on lorry drivers in the main to get me there and back. I travelled ticketless on the trains for most of the way although I remember being caught by a guard near Oxford and borrowing money from a passenger for the last leg of the journey, leaving something as security. I think it was a fountain pen.

All was well with my family so after a night's sleep I began the return journey by road. Lifts were fairly easy to come by until, again near Oxford, we were halted at an army control point. No leave pass meant immediate arrest and I was confined within a Pioneer Corps bell tent of First World War vintage whilst arrangements were being made for an RAF escort to arrive and transport me back to Blackpool. We went by train and I sat for the whole trip in handcuffs with two armed Corporals of the RAF Police as my guards.

On, arrival in Blackpool, I was taken to a Police Station where I spent the night in a cell and, next morning, I appeared before the commanding officer who told me that they were considering the charge of <u>Desertion</u> and did I know the penalty for such an offence in time of war?

I just blurted out about the Air Raid and about Mum and Dad and my sisters. I remember being almost in tears telling the C.O. that I had only enlisted a few months earlier and all I wanted to do was fly with the RAF. I rushed out about the journey and how I was well on the way back when my luck deserted me. I really was not 'deserting' as such. After consultation with other officers on the Bench he said that I would be charged as being 'Absent without Leave' and that my punishment would be 14 days 'Confined to Barracks' but <u>not</u> in Blackpool.

I was to serve the sentence when we moved on to our next Station. This proved to be RAF Cranwell, the home of the Royal Air Force and probably the strictest station in the UK. This part of my training ended ignominiously but I was so relieved not to have faced the much more serious charge that I was not in the least concerned about what might lay in store at No.1 Signals School, Cranwell, Lincs.

Training RAF Cranwell, Lincs
No.1 Signals School (Section 2)

This was another period of training in Wireless Telegraphy, advancing my Morse code speed from what seemed an incredibly fast 12 words per minute up to 22 w.p.m. and finally right up to 26 w.p.m.

Nearly three and a half months from the 14th February through to the 24th May 1941 now followed.

Only a handful of Blackpool's Class 1c12 made the journey to Cranwell, the remainder being posted to other training centres such as Yatesbury in Wiltshire.I became part of Course 1AG5E and a whole new raft of friendships evolved.

Of the twenty on the course, there developed a close knit inner circle of eight; Jaker, Ben, Len, Jeff, Doug, Mac, Bill and myself. This, as it happens, proved not to be such a brilliant idea. Four of them failed to survive subsequent schooling at their Operational Training Unit (OTU) final tutelage. Before joining a front line squadron, Ben, Len, Jeff, and Bill were all killed in crashes in aeroplanes piloted by young inexperienced pilots. Jaker, Doug, Mac and I at least survived OTU.

However, we knew nothing of what the future might hold and our relationships grew stronger by the day. The course even had its own football team, mainly comprising seven of our coterie. I acted as coach, cheer leader, linesman, ball boy, in fact in any capacity other than that of a player. Football was not a King Edward's sport. Now if it had been Rugby.........!

Course 1AG5E football team at Cranwell May 1941. Author standing left back row

But before all this, was the punishment, the '14 days Confined to Barracks' to survive. Our training days were long and intense and evening study was necessary. This now had to be fitted in around rising at some unearthly hour to report in full, spotless uniform, at the Station Guard House in time to be standing at attention alongside the Bugler as he sounded 'Reveille'. Many domestic tasks followed - sweeping, cleaning windows, dusting, clearing out the fire grate and re-laying the fire, running messages for the guards and, last but not least, cleaning their rifles and equipment.

You were allowed just enough time to race to the airmen's mess, bolt down a quick, late and often not very hot breakfast, before dashing to the lecture room. At lunch time you fitted in a meal around a further stint at the guardroom, getting back to your studies with seconds to spare.

You had no evening. Immediately after training you reported to the guardroom, where a dozen tasks awaited you. Apart from a short break whilst you raced to the Mess for a meal and back, you were available to the guards and duty officers until you stood by the bugler, late at night, as he sounded 'Lights out' or was it the 'Last Post'? You then had to find your way back in the dark to your hut, albeit in a strange camp, have a few hours sleep, then back on to the treadmill. It proved to be the longest two weeks of my life; interminable. For the rest of the war I toed the party line.

The time came when we were becoming really proficient and, early in May, we were issued with our first flying suits. One can still re-capture the inner excitement. The thrill, the mood of walking on air experienced by this super group of young friends, mainly teenagers, as Sidcot suits were issued, along with helmets and goggles, long leather gauntlets and of course the inevitable flying boots.

All 'Togged Up'. Back row: Jaker, Ben, Len, Author. Front row: Jeff, Doug, Mac and Bill after being issued with flying kit at Cranwell in May 1941

You can sense the atmosphere when you see an old photograph of the eight of us, all togged up; some with flying helmets and goggles. The inane grin on one or two of our faces says it all, total, almost delirious joy. 'We are about to become real airmen, we are about to fly!'

In fact, the actual flying training period only lasted from the 1st to the 6th May when I flew in a Vickers Valentia, a de-Havilland Rapide and a Percival Proctor.

My very first flight was of 30 minutes duration in the Rapide on May 1st 1941, still only aged seventeen. I made two flights on the 2nd May, one hour ten minutes in the morning and an hour and a half in the afternoon. On the 3rd May another two flights, each of about half an hour. Then on the 4th May, a total of six flights, averaging about thirty minutes each. On the 5th May, another five of similar duration whilst on the final day, the 6th May, I was airborne for half an hour, then for one and a half hours. My instructor's comments ranged from 'good' through to 'satisfactory' to 'very good'.

Sending and receiving Morse code messages at over 20 words per minute in a smelly, noisy, vibrating aeroplane, which most certainly did not fly straight and level as do today's huge jets, was extremely difficult for us beginners. Both the Rapide and the Proctor seemed to be floating on a turbulent sea, constantly rising and falling, whilst the late 1920s Vickers Valentia induced air sickness in most of the young wireless operators.

Notwithstanding the difficulties, we all duly passed sufficient of the many tests. Then came the great moment when our WOP arm badge was ceremoniously awarded.

Finally, on the 24th May at the end of the course, I was promoted to the rank of Aircraftman First Class/Wireless Operator and thus became an AC1/WOP with an increase in my daily pay from 2/6d to 4/9d (today, just under 25 pence per day.)

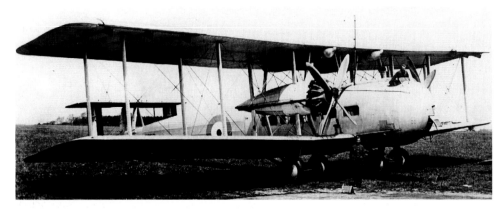

The very same Valentia K3601 that the auther flew in, pictured here at Cranwell before the outbreak of the Second World War

A few days before we left Cranwell, the war landed on our doorstep. It was a German aeroplane, fighter? bomber? I know not what, (it all happened too quickly). It appeared at the end of the airfield, came in very low and machine gunned our training planes, fortunately without causing too much damage. The noise and confusion, added to the sheer shock of witnessing at first hand the reality of war was, for some, quite overwhelming. I can remember dropping to the ground, then running, only to realise the plane was coming in again for a second attack and stopping to watch. It was mesmeric, almost fascinating, and I remember thinking that perhaps one day soon I would be able to repeat this against a German airfield.

End of Course 1AG5E photo in May 1941

On 'leaving' day, we were yet again issued with the inevitable travel warrants and rations for the journey to - no, not to Air Gunnery School, but once more to 'marking time' tasks. This time with the Signals Section at RAF Benson in Oxfordshire.

Training RAF Benson, Oxon
(Photographic Reconnaissance Squadrons)
(Section 3)

I have little or no recollection of my time at this airfield from the 7th June to the 5th July 1941 so our existence there must have been pretty humdrum. Probably not boring though, with the aircraft of Photo Reconnaissance squadrons flying out on extremely dangerous missions. The vast majority at the time were along the coastline of mainland Europe, over the Norwegian harbours and even inland; there would always have been news of their exploits leaking out of the Ops Room.

Sufficient to say that in less than a month we were again 'on the move', this time to the most eagerly awaited Air Gunnery School at Penrhos, Gwynedd, North West Wales, armed as usual with travel warrant and rations for the journey.

Training
No.9 Bombing and Gunnery School, Penrhos, North Wales
(Section 4)

There now followed three weeks of sheer bliss, from the 5th to the 26th July 1941, enhanced on the third day when I was promoted to the dizzy rank of Leading Aircraftsman and entitled to wear the propeller badge on my arm. Best of all, though, my daily rate of pay increased from 4/9d to 6/6d. (Equivalent to 32½ pence).

The majority of our training was in the classroom or workshop learning about guns. From the 14th to the 24th July, I made four flights in Fairey Battles and one in a Bristol Blenheim, each about three quarters of an hour duration. They were all Air-to-Air Gunnery exercises, firing at towed drogues.

I started off with just 50 rounds, progressing up to 400 rounds on my last flight at the school. My final report, printed in my flying log book, registers examination marks of 75% and in the remarks section is recorded 'A promising Air Gunner'.

I have few other memories of our time at Penrhos, other than that we were billeted in a private house in a wee village away from the airfield called Llanbedrog and that the beaches in the vicinity were superb.So I will quote a few extracts from 'Toward the Sun', a book written in novel style, purporting to be fictional but based on the detailed records my fellow WOP/AG and current friend, Richard Thomas, must have kept at the time.

"The Vickers 0.303 machine gun, a beautiful weapon. How to strip it down, to name its component parts and re-assemble it".

Then, in the air, firing at the drogues

"The roar of the Vickers shattered his eardrums despite the protection afforded by his flying helmet"

Writing of the Fairey Battles. Firing from an open cockpit might look the part in a film like 'Hell's Angels' but in actual fact it was fraught with hazards."

Towards the end of our three week stay in Wales, we were assembled in one of the lecture rooms to discuss our future roles. We were each given the opportunity to express a desire to fly in a particular type of plane when we began operations. The majority seemed to plump for Wellingtons, Hampdens, Beaufighters and other sundry aircraft employed in Bomber Command raids.

By this time, our group of eight at Cranwell had been dispersed and I had chummed up with a fellow WOP/AG, Joe Peet of Nottingham. I can clearly remember him nudging me and whispering that he had heard of some American planes now becoming available to the RAF that they were made of metal, not fabric like the Wellington, and that perhaps they might be safer. He thought they were called Lockheeds, so when it came to our turn we both opted for the 'Lockheed' without having a clue as to what they were like, what tasks were performed in them or where they were flown from. And so one's destiny was determined and whether or not you would survive the war, was set in stone; Thank You, Joe.

Then, on the 26th July 1941, I was awarded my Air Gunner Brevet and, on being promoted to the rank of Sergeant, the three stripes for the arms of my uniform tunic. At the time I must have been among the youngest Sergeants in the whole of the Air Force, at 18 years and 2 months. How proud I felt and, hastened to stitch them all in place. Equally exciting, my daily rate of pay increased to 7/9d. (Just under 40 pence a day!)

Then we were on our way yet again; this time to Cumbria, to RAF Silloth, for quite a long stay. Our operational training there was to be the prelude to 'going on ops'. At last our training was reaching a climax.

Chapter 4
Training Silloth 1 OTU

ometime after leaving Silloth, I came across the slogan; "IF YOU SURVIVE OTU YOU WILL SURVIVE THE WAR". As it happened, I survived both, but far too many lost their lives at Operational Training Units.

At the Silloth unit alone nearly seventy Lockheed Hudsons were lost on non operational flying during the 1941/43 periods. It was almost one a fortnight. About fifteen in 1941 (three on our course alone), thirty six in 1942 and seventeen in 1943. There were crashed landings, crashes on take off, crashes into hillsides and ditching into the sea. In fact, so many had ditched into the Solway Firth that it became known as 'Hudson Bay'.

Most of this detail came to hand much later; during my two month stay such depressing statistics were not published. Even the three fatal crashes in August and September were played down and any information we gained came from rumours. There were no public announcements about any of them. You just realised that some of your friends were not around any more. In any case, you were too wrapped up with your own problems arising out of the intensive training. We were so busy each and every day in the classroom, in the air or on the Square, drilling and more drilling so that it was not easy to take on board the rumours.

I suppose that one's mechanism tended to shut out such bad tidings, to enable you to carry on. Thinking about the possibility that you might be next was just <u>not</u> permissible. You really did have to concentrate on one thing only and that had to be your training for war.

When I first arrived at Silloth for the two month course on the 29th July, I was disturbed to find hardly any of 1AG5E on this new period of training, maybe there were valid reasons. Perhaps most of them had gone to Bomber Command OTUs!

So began the forging of new friendships and Joe and I seemed well-suited. We knew that we would need to find ourselves a couple of pilot/navigators so Joe proposed an early study of those still available. He said we needed to locate two who appeared to be on friendly terms with each other, quiet, studious-looking types. Preferably they needed to be non drinkers

No.9 Hudson Operations Course, No.1 OTU Silloth August 1941

and not too adventurous looking. His theory was that, as our lives were to be placed in their hands, we needed to find two pairs of safe hands.

When we espied Alan and Les we just knew they were to be the ones, so we approached them and offered the services of the two best wireless ops and air gunners on the course!! We gelled at once and duly registered as a crew with the flight commander.

During the first month, the pilots, who had just arrived from Flying Training Schools, had to learn how to fly a twin engine aircraft. This was a massive step from the dinky single engine types they had grown used to, often in Canada or Rhodesia. They must have done dozens and dozens of take offs and landings, trying to master the idiosyncrasies of the Lockheed Hudson.

The first months for the WOP/AGs comprised flights in Avro Ansons and Airspeed Oxfords. Performing exercises in establishing two way W/T communications, frequency changes, MF/DF positions, HF/MF bearings, R/T communication, reply by W/T etc, I enjoyed a 72% Pass rate.

These exercises were spread over twenty two days and we flew on twelve of them, fourteen flights with eight different pilots. The non-flying days were on the barrack square or in the classroom.

Only three of the pilots who flew us during this first half of our stay at Silloth were Sergeants. All the others ranged from pilot officers up to flight lieutenants, suggesting that they were very experienced men, probably on rest after an initial operational tour during the very early part of the war.

As we moved into the second month, we flew as a crew and only in the Lockheed Hudson. We squeezed in 43 flights in the 25 flying days available, sometimes flying three, even four,

All marks of the Hudson were flown by 1 OTU at Silloth, including the Mk.V shown here

sorties in a 24 hour period. Nearly a third of the flights were in the dark. This was a frighteningly high proportion when you recognise our overall inexperience.

There were so very many things to learn;

High and low level bombing	Night navigation
Periscope bombing	Two way R/T communication
Turret manipulation	Navigation exercises of 3-4 hours duration
Air/ground and splash firing	Evening sighting and 'not met' reports
Pilots' gunnery	Frequency check and change Loop bearings
Search techniques	MF/MF Fixes

Bearing in mind that most of the courses exercises were repeated in more advanced form as the course progressed. The amount of time and care invested in the crews by the instructors was immense. Although they were always on hand, they allowed our two pilots to captain twenty six of the twenty nine day flights, only assuming command when major air gunner or pilot firing was being undertaken.

At night, nine of the fourteen flights were captained by instructors, there was an introductory flight and, after this, eight acclimatisation flights of fairly short duration which were mainly concerned with take-off and landing procedures. The final five were made with just the crew, the four of us, on board. They were of much longer duration, in effect, night navigation exercises. They usually lasted three to four hours.

Altogether I registered 107 flying hours at Silloth. We had accumulated a grand total of 121 hours since flying training began at Signals School, we thought we were ready for 'operations' and were duly posted to Coastal Command, 206 Squadron, then based at Aldergrove, County Antrim, Northern Ireland.

But before I move onto this, I would comment further on the losses of crews and aeroplanes at Silloth.

Firstly, of the 24 different Hudsons I flew in at No.1 OTU, only twelve survived the war. Of the other 50%, ten crashed on take off or landing, one ditched in the Solway Firth and another was damaged beyond repair in a taxiing accident.

During the August and September of 1941, our time at Silloth, three of our Hudsons and crews were lost. One crash landed, one ditched off Grune Point and the third crashed into a hill near Ramsey, IOM but we knew none of this detail at the time. These were our friends. They never 'made it' as we said, and one had no option but to be sad for a while and then carry on as before, knowing and believing 100% that it would not happen to you. It was certainly a relief when we left Silloth, OTU.

In the years after the war, there were many investigations into aircraft losses in training, in all Commands. Apart from known problems with the planes themselves, the phrase 'massively undertrained', applied to the pilots by post war standards, says it all. Well, there was no time was there? In the hackneyed phrase 'There was a war on'.

Aircrew of all nations lie side by side in the cemetery to the south of the airfield at Silloth. 56 graves of the airmen who did not make it through their flying training at No. 1 OTU. (Martyn Chorlton)

Chapter 5

Operations, Aldergrove, Northern Ireland

I t was the 2nd October before I arrived at Aldergrove. I had probably enjoyed a few days leave after departing from Silloth and, along with Alan, Les and Joe, I was posted to 'A' Flight under the Command of Flt Lt R.C. Patrick.

On the 4th October 1941, my first flight out of Aldergrove was in a Hudson AM605, piloted by an experienced Flt Sgt Gibbs. We made a 1½ hour familiarisation trip around the local area so that Joe and I could become accustomed to using the turret, handling the guns and operating the radio. It had similar equipment to the Silloth machines but this time the aircraft was fully operational with live ammunition.

This causes me to reflect on my final flight out of Aldergrove which was on the 30th June 1942, nine months later, in a Hudson AM822. It was an hour and three quarters flight to Benbecula in the Outer Hebrides. The squadron was necessarily transferred to the Western Isles, as the Battle of the Atlantic had moved into more Northern Latitudes, enabling us to provide greater coverage for the increasing numbers of convoys crossing and re-crossing that mighty ocean in both directions. But that was far in the future.

Reverting back to Aldergrove and our arrival, we duly settled into life in the wooden hut that we were to call home for these nine months, just the same as we had done previously on other RAF Stations.

There was a lot you could do really, just check that there were the correct number of blankets and pillows, that you had a mattress, a bedside cabinet and a shelf. Then it was merely a case of tipping out your kit-bag, finding space to hang your uniforms and stowing your underclothes, boots, toiletries, etc.

Finally it was down to the Sergeants' Mess to find out if any of the other Silloth crews were there and, if not, thinking about which squadron they had been posted to. We then checked out the NAAFI, as it was there that we would obtain all the little extras; not only endless cups of tea but also cakes, sandwiches, chocolate (when available) and the 101 other items such as toothpaste and shaving cream.

Ah yes! Shaving cream, not a product I needed to spend my hard-earned pennies on, as shaving had not then become necessary. I cannot remember when I first wielded a razor but even today I can occasionally skip a day's shaving and no one seems to notice. 'Tis all in the genes!

The existence and actual presence of the NAAFI (The Navy, Army and Air Force Institute) had a considerable bearing on the morale of all non commissioned ranks and I doubt if there was a single serviceman who was not constantly grateful to the organisation.

Our first evening in the Sergeants Mess proved to be quite disturbing. After the evening meal we young, newly-promoted Sergeants were invited to a so-called 'Introduction Ceremony'.

We were lined up along one side of trestle tables that were placed end to end and covered with large white tablecloths. Opposite each one of us was a long service NCO, maybe a sergeant, a flight sergeant or even a warrant officer; most of them with probably ten to twenty years service and having served most of that time in the ranks which was a very long period indeed before reaching their present levels. Not just a few brief months like the aircrew opposite them.

A pint of beer was placed in front of each participating NCO and thence began a drinking race to ascertain which side of the table would see their pints consumed first. The outcome was obvious. I doubt if our young Sergeants team had even reached the half way mark when the other side had downed their final pint.

We than paid the loser's penalty. I remember being politely escorted outside, my trousers and underpants being removed and a smear of mustard being applied to my testicles. The pain was excruciating. Obviously a health warning needs to be recorded - 'DO NOT TRY THIS AT HOME!'

In the event, I suppose most of the senior NCO's felt that they had made their point and established their superiority. It was never talked about afterwards and I cannot remember there being any hard feelings on either side in the ensuing weeks and months. Any idea that we had 'finished' training soon vanished, as we quickly discovered that, when not on operational flying, training filled a large part of the day.

My second flight, on the 6th, in AM587, consisted of acting as R/T operator to Les as he carried out a series of 'Circuits and Bumps'. Literally taking off, circling the airfield and then landing; taxiing back to the other end of the runway and doing it all over again and again and again. We never gave a thought to his being a relatively inexperienced pilot. Guess we probably thought that he was a pilot, so he must be safe to fly with!

Then, on the 8th, less than a week after joining the squadron, I embarked on my very first operational flight, in a Hudson AM622, with an experienced pilot, Sgt Ireland and a WOP/AG. It is possible that either Les or Alan was the co-pilot. It was not a very auspicious start to the 'real thing', we returned after half an hour with a faulty radio. After the necessary repair, we took off again on an Anti-Sub Sweep, only to return once more after only four hours due to the appalling visibility out at sea. Joe Peet would have flown a similar trip with our other pilot, an experienced captain and a WOP/AG.

A week later, again with Sgt Ireland as captain, we set out to find and escort a convoy and carried out an Anti-Sub Patrol around it. After another four days, Sgt Ireland took us

RAF Aldergrove during 206 Squadrons tour in 1942

out to find a convoy threatened with air attack. However, we had to return as the weather conditions were again so bad that we were unable to locate it.

Two days later, with the same crew, we headed north west, found the convoy and carried out Anti-sub Patrols as directed by the Naval Escort. Maximum airborne time in those early days was about 6½ hours. My log book records this exactly, so we could not have had much fuel left.

In between these Ops trips we would fly out on Navigation Exercises, usually to Rockall, or to RAF Airfields. The training included practice dive bombing and photography, night flights over Belfast, dropping flares from 10,000 feet to test the City's smoke screen and air to sea firing with either Sgt Ireland or our C.O., Wg Cdr Hards, as Captain for this particular aspect. We also squeezed in 'Circuits and Bumps' for Alan, for over an hour. Just think how many times we took off and landed in the evening light!

I did two more Ops flights with Sgt Ireland, the first as convoy escort with the usual Anti-Sub Patrol, the second as escort to a single MV (Merchant Vessel) which had become 'lost'; a convoy straggler and thus very prone to U-Boat attack. Our task was to try and persuade her onto the correct course to rejoin her convoy, meantime, by our very presence, keeping any marauding U-Boat at bay.

On the last day of October, at the end of our first month of operational flying, we spent a pleasant hour or so firing hundreds of rounds at airborne towed drogues. It was training, but great fun, even though it was extremely noisy.

November dawned, and on the second day we flew on our first ops mission as a crew, Alan, Les, Joe and I, escorting an aircraft carrier on a six hour flight.

It was quite a moving experience and, once away from Ireland and right out of sight of land, we began to appraise ourselves. An amazing sense of realism affected us all. For the first time, we recognised the immense weight of responsibility that lay on our young shoulders.

There we were, heading out above the North Atlantic in a huge American aircraft, loaded down with fuel, depth charges, cannon, machine guns, belts of ammunition and some food and drink - on our own with no operationally experienced pilot on board to guide us. With our training over so very many months, we only had to ensure that we followed correct procedures and would be able to handle any emergency.

We had to walk away from the inescapable fact that our average age was under twenty and that, included the very young WOP/AG Ted Nelson who was still only eighteen and a half. We just had to accept that both he and Joe Peet were top class wireless operators. No one could dispute my personal best of 26 words per minute, sending and receiving Morse, and there was no doubt about our visual abilities. With 20/20, vision we knew that if there was a submarine on the surface, or even if only at conning tower level, we would sight it. We were confident in our abilities to accurately fire any of the guns on board and to quickly remedy any fault.

Then, away in the distance, we sighted our aircraft carrier and all these nervous thoughts left us. We were on the job, fully trained and as we grew close enough, we were able to signal with our Aldis Lamp and identify ourselves.

It was so easy to imagine the number of naval gunners called to 'Action Stations' on the sighting of our aircraft, as we could so easily have been a hostile one. There were perceptible sighs of relief when the carrier acknowledged our signal.

This same sense of relief was felt by the crews of every single aircraft involved in any form of liaison with the Navy. All WOP/AG's were most keen to ensure that their lamp flashing identification skills were kept well honed. They knew their lives could depend on it as the Navy were quite rightly very, very nervous of approaching aircraft.

We duly searched the area in front of the carrier, the area astern and finally the port and starboard sections. Settling down to a 'Creeping Line Ahead', we then searched in the various areas that we were directed to by the carrier. We were later relieved by another Hudson and its crew and flew east, back to Ireland and to safety.

Later on in the month, several hours were spent combing Lough Eyre, searching for the crew of a 'missing' Hudson (not from our squadron) which had 'Failed to Return', but without success. On our own safe return, we flew very low down the Bann Valley. The River Bann runs roughly north-south and, by picking it up on the north coast at Portstewart, one could follow it south to Lough Neagh and thence to Aldergrove.

Sgt. E. H. Nelson 1181644

Xmas, 1941.

| SHQ | 206 SQDN | 1402 | 1405 | 143 SQDN | GOPF |

Sergeants' Mess, Aldergrove.

Menu.

Soup.
Cream of Celery.

Fish and Tomato Sauce.

Roast Turkey..............
Baked Ham and Stuffing...
Brussels Sprouts..........
Baked Potatoes...........

Xmas Pudding with Brandy Sauce..........

Mince Pies......
Apples....

Cigarettes..... Beer.

A Merry Xmas!

Whizzing down it at some speed and not always above tree top height was an exhilarating experience and a great relief after the tension and concentration of an ops flight. It was not dissimilar to 'beating up' the airfield on occasion. But on this particular whiz we so very nearly 'bought it'. Fortunately, Les proved his worth as a pilot when we were struck, either by a single large bird or by a small flock. The astro dome and turret were smashed and the inside mid area and tail became a mess of bird, feathers and mangled flesh and bone. Somehow, Les maintained control of the aircraft and rapidly gained height before continuing to Aldergrove at a safer and less adventurous altitude.

We were desperately unpopular with the ground crew who had to sort out the 'bloody' mess and with the C.O. who was desperately short of serviceable aircraft at that time. Fortunately, however, there were no bad lines on our records, as it was claimed to be 'accidental damage'.

The weather then deteriorated so much that we did not fly from the 17th November until the 5th December and, even then we had to return after three quarters of an hour because conditions were too rough. This was followed by a flight up to Wick, in the north east corner of Scotland, to bring back a Hudson that had become stranded there. It was the 8th, (three days later), before we could return from therebecause by then conditions had worsened. Even then the flight took three hours. On the 10th, we were flown over to Hawarden to catch a train south for a well-earned ten days leave.

We were back 'in harness' before Christmas and, in fact on Christmas Eve we carried out a full six hour Anti-Sub sweep over the North Atlantic. Christmas Day lasts just one day at such times and, on the 27th and 28th, we were out doing low level practice bombing on Lough Neagh. Firstly with Alan as Captain and then with Les in the hot seat

We lost two of our aircraft in December. AM634 ditched whilst on patrol on the 11th and AM837 literally 'Failed to Return' from another patrol on the 21st. Eight more of our friends, the crews, all perished, bringing to 16 the squadron's total aircraft losses in the year. Our odds were shortening.

1942 started little better, with five losses in the first forty five days. January was a very busy month. We managed seven ops flights, twice as convoy escort, the others either as Anti-Sub Sweeps or Special Searches. On two occasions, bad weather forced us to return after only four or five hours. We also fitted in eighteen non ops flights, mainly training exercises, including;

Navigation exercise	Formation flying, nine aircraft.
Low Level Bombing (four sessions)	Defending against mock attacks by Spitfire
Air/Ground Gunnery	and also by Gladiator.
Local night flying (dual then single)	Pilots Air to Sea Firing
Practice dive bombing on cruiser	A one hour flight to Hawarden, (going on
HMS *Charybadis*	leave on the 28th).
Compass Swinging (four flights)	

We were soon back on duty and, on the 9th February, we were deployed up to Stornoway on the east coast of the Isle of Harris, in the Western Isles, for an Anti-Sub sweep on the 10th. It took us over two and a half hours to fly from Northern Ireland to Stornoway. How times have changed, I imagine it would take less than an hour nowadays. We returned to

206 Squadron at Aldergrove on the 21st April 1942. From the left; Joe Peet, Les Goodson, Ted Nelson and Alan Marriott

Aldergrove in time to provide the Anti-sub escort to five ships, part of a convoy that had scattered after a U-boat attack.

Then, on St. Valentine's Day, it all went 'pear shaped'. We were to be undertaking our usual type of Anti-sub sweep with an 06:45 take off in the dark. Les was not actually qualified for night flying at Aldergrove as he had not taken off and landed enough times at night under supervision.

Without giving it full consideration, Alan asked Joe and me if we would be agreeable to Les taking the controls for take off. We automatically concurred as we had flown plenty of times with Les as Captain, even though they had only involved daytime take offs and landings. How wrong could we be?

At any rate, we duly prepared for take off with Joe up front, close by the two pilots and me, standing up, looking out of the astro dome half way down the fuselage. We bid farewell on the R/T to the young WAAF on duty inside the Control Tower. We then continued chatting as the aircraft raced down the runway. (None of us were 'strapped in'.)

Now whether Les, a god-fearing man, was troubled by his conscience or whether he left it a wee bit too late to pull back on the controls I will never know. If the matter had been discussed it would have been when I was in hospital.

Whatever the reason, we left it too late to become properly airborne, became tangled with some electricity cabling and crashed into a field. Les and Alan climbed out of the emergency hatch above the flight deck, quickly followed by Joe Peet. They each slid down the port wing and dropped to the ground. The starboard engine was on fire. Neither of the pilots could open the main fuselage door but Joe, with his extra strength and one of his feet braced against the fuselage, was more successful. He leapt in and found me crumpled up in the rear of the aircraft, where I had been thrown by the impact. The poor WAAF on the other end of the R/T link must have been quite concerned when the conversation came to such an abrupt end. The Control Tower staff later said that from take off to final explosion was about twenty six/twenty seven seconds.

Joe dragged me out, by which time the port engine was also ablaze. The three of them then pulled me at great speed along the ground and into a ditch. I can remember being quite tearful. Shock I suppose, but I blurted out that I was crying because we had left the pigeons behind. In those days, we used to take a couple in a brown wicker basket to send back 'submarine sighted' messages in case of radio failure or poor transmission conditions.

The explosion was huge as tanks full of fuel and a bomb bay loaded with depth charges finally succumbed to the heat generated by the two burning engines. I never saw the hole in the ground that was all that remained as I was being taken to a Belfast hospital. The fire engine arrived, the C.O's car appeared and Alan, Les and Joe were hastily returned to the airfield. They were bundled into another aircraft and flown out by the C.O. himself to prove to them that aircraft really could become airborne if flown properly.

Apparently, the three agreed not to let on about Les, with Alan accepting full pilot responsibility for the crash. He was duly punished with the awful offence of 'pilot error' and his career was blighted for some time. In the longer term, he stayed on in the RAF after the war, did a spell as a Test Pilot and, at one time, so I am told, was the commanding officer at Gibraltar.

Les had problems and left the squadron before our move to Benbecula. I heard that he survived a mid-air collision but was badly burned. Neither Alan nor Les nor even Joe Peet lived to a ripe old age and I count my blessings day by day.

After a stay in hospital with the usual cuts and bruises and a broken arm, probably followed by a spot of sick leave, it was a whole month before I was airborne again. On the 17th March I went on four local flights, one with Alan as pilot. We flew again as a crew the next day completing a series of 'Circuits and Bumps' to get us all used to the idea of safely taking off and landing, time and time again.

Finally, on the 24th, we were back on ops, yet another Anti-Sub Sweep. It is of particular note that it was Les, who was now No.1, the captain, and his promotion to the rank of Flight Sergeant was well received. Our last ops trip in March was on the 29th in AM788, a fairly standard Anti-Sub sweep but in such appalling weather that we were forced back after

Lockheed Hudson I 'VX-B' of 206 Squadron. [via Martyn Chorlton]

The good functional and relatively spacious cockpit of a Lockheed Hudson. [269 Sqn records via Martyn Chorlton]

only four hours. Even then we had to land at Limavady, (near Londonderry) as Aldergrove was closed in, zero cloud base.

In between the 24th and 29th, we enjoyed several training flights; Air-to-Sea firing from side and rear guns, from front guns and also some practice low level bombing. It was great fun for an Air Gunner to be allowed to fire off hundreds of rounds and then, a couple of days later, to do it all again. It's quite exhilarating too when the C.O. takes over and, from two or three thousand feet, dives the aircraft down with the front guns blasting. The noise is quite intense but, for a young lad, still aged eighteen, a most exciting experience.

There were several more ops flights in April, mainly Anti-sub sweeps, and with different Captains on some of them; so far not with Alan. We then seemed to be airborne for up to seven hours on occasions.

One of our Sweeps was from Tiree in the Western Isles, flying up there on the 29th and taking off again for the op at 21:00 hours. Did it stay light much later up there or were we beginning to use ASV Radar?

During the month, there were plenty more training flights, particularly low level bombing, but also co-operating with the army searchlight teams. We were flying here and there at 12,000 feet whilst they tried to locate us. Again, it was great fun, but quite spooky when you were caught in the full glare of several beams simultaneously. We also enjoyed a spot of formation flying.

On the 8th, T9431 crashed on take off, it was our sixth casualty so far that year. May 1942 was another very busy month with seven ops flights; mainly Anti-Sub sweeps, one of which lasted nearly eight hours, on another we were forced to land at Limavady again due to weather problems at Aldergrove. On the 18th, we experienced life at 18,000 feet in

Author's best friend Joe Peet who was shot down on the 1000-bomber raid to Bremen in June 1942

an unheated aeroplane. It was probably the coldest I have ever been, despite our fur-lined leather flying suits, padded boots and three pairs of gloves; a seven hour twenty minute meteorological flight towards the mid-Atlantic.

On the 24th May, I was flown over to Ballykelly for my three days on the destroyer HMS *Keppel*, returning from Eglinton. The full story is in Chapter 6.

Earlier in the month, we fitted in flights to Bircham Newton and to Grantham as well as two sessions of local night flying and a low level bombing trip with new pilots. On our first attempt to fly to Bircham Newton on the 17th, with Les in charge, we lost power in the port engine. Once again, however, he came up trumps and returned us safely to Aldergrove with an emergency one engine landing after being airborne for fifteen minutes. Two and a half hours later, we took off in the same (repaired) aircraft and delivered it safely to the Norfolk RAF Station two and three quarters hours later.

It is worth recording that, at the end of the month, our aircraft were repainted ready for attachment to Bomber Command for the first 1000 bomber raid on Cologne. The critical situation which was developing in the Atlantic precluded this trip however and the aircraft had to be re-camouflaged.

Then came the busy month of June, our last month at Aldergrove, with the usual Anti-Sub Sweeps as well as my longest ever Hudson flight of nine and three quarter hours. We were acting as Anti-Aircraft Escort to a convoy expecting an air attack so I guess we left behind the depth charges, replacing them with extra fuel tanks. On our return, the paint shop again took over and soon our normally bright Hudsons were blackened in readiness for Bomber Command support.

On the 23rd June, we flew east to North Coates, Lincs, and in the evening made the short flight to a satellite field at Donna Nook. Tragically, we damaged an Oleo Leg on landing and our aircraft thus became unserviceable. Not to be outdone, the four of us were each allowed to select another crew to fly with and I joined up with Fg Off Eric Bland.

On the 25th, with a thousand other aircraft, we flew out over the North Sea, heading for the German city of Bremen. It was truly was an unbelievable sight, in every direction there were aircraft as far as the eye could see. Black shapes silhouetted against the night sky.

The overall flight lasted six hours and thirty five minutes and was packed with incidents. One's first sight of flak and of anti-aircraft fire was quite exciting. It was all so colourful, so concentrated, yet we seemed to pass it by in the early stages. The closer we flew to Bremen the more intense it became until, finally, we reached our target.

I will never, ever, forget my first sighting of a German city in flames, with super-bright searchlights weaving around and an aerial firework display produced by the exploding Ack Ack shells. The whole scene was hypnotic and it was only the calm voice of the pilot, Eric Bland, talking to the Navigator/Bomb Aimer on the bombing run that brought one back to reality and made me realise that this had nothing to do with Guy Fawkes. This was for real!

One marveled at the way so many aircraft could be concentrated in one area and yet not collide, and that the bursting shells did not seem to be hitting the aircraft. We were so very fortunate as far too many shells did find their target. In fact, forty eight of the total force 'Failed to Return'. We stayed long enough to complete our bombing run and to see hundreds of explosions on the ground. Then our Skipper did the sensible thing and set course for England. (How our flight ended is detailed in Chapter 8).

206 Squadron aircrew at Aldergrove in April 1942

On the 27th, we returned to Aldergrove and on the 29th did a return flight to Benbecula. The following day, we again flew up to Benbecula, this time to stay; our nine month stint at Aldergrove had come to an end. We had flown 35 Ops, totalling over 200 hours plus dozens of non-ops trips totalling about 100 hours. And last but by no means least, eleven lost aircraft and crews in the nine months, two of them over Bremen.

Well, nearly last, as before finally leaving Northern Ireland here is a brief comment on 'The Troubles'.Generally speaking, we tend to think of the end of the 1960s, the

1970s and the 1980s, but I can remember walking through the streets of Belfast fairly late at night, with Alan, Les and Joe, accompanying our two pilot's dance partners, escorting them home in fact. There was just a moment, when I heard one of the girls recommending that we cross over the road to avoid certain streets nearby. It was there that we had our first encounter with 'the problem'. So even in late 1941, early 1942 there was animosity, in Belfast at least. What would Benbecula now have in store for us?

Sgt WOP/AG Ted Nelson June 1942

Chapter 6
Aboard HMS *Keppel*, 1942

A fter just eight months on 206 Squadron at Aldergrove, I was flown over to RAF Ballykelly by Flt Sgt Hill in Hudson N7225 on the evening of the 21st May; a thirty minute flight. I was then taken by road to Londonderry to join an operational destroyer of the North Atlantic fleet, HMS *Keppel*.

Senior officers of the Western Approaches must have been feeling that there was a need for closer integration of crews at the 'sharp end', a need for more liaisons between the sailors of the Royal Navy and the airmen of the Royal Air Force.

I was to be the sacrificial lamb that had to brave the Atlantic in a front line naval vessel and report back on how this closer liaison could be achieved in future months. It was genuinely felt by HQ-types that such interchanges of personnel would improve the understanding between the two services and thus improve co-operation on and above the Atlantic.

After leaving the habour, there was a torpedo firing and recovery exercise and as I watched, from the deck, I felt so pleased that I had succeeded in joining the RAF and not the Navy.

A cup-shaped receptacle in the nose of each torpedo belched out a most obnoxious smelling cloud of smoke as its contents were swamped with sea water. (Was it carbide?) As a result, there was no difficulty in locating the whereabouts of each 'tin fish'.

Ratings in the water had to loop a couple of cables around the torpedo so that it could be landed aboard. This was no easy task in a choppy sea and with a choking, swirling cloud streaming from the nose of the torpedo where the cable loops had to be forced over and then tightened.

The petty officer who was supervising the recovery was not at all sympathetic and his bellowed commands and shouted abuse hardly seemed to encourage the swimmers; more the reverse.

I was greatly relieved when the operation was complete and we were able to head for our rendezvous with the cruiser that we were to escort into the Atlantic. Cruisers travel quite fast and our destroyer seemed to be racing at full speed just to keep up with her.

The long-serving HMS Keppel a Shakespeare Class Flotilla Leader launched back in 1920

The Queen Mary at full throttle in the North Atlantic on the 2nd October 1942

It was just after dawn on the second day when I looked out of a port hole in the Petty Officers Mess and, after initially sighting nothing but incredibly high seas, I suddenly espied a huge liner racing at great speed through the mountainous waves. I looked around at the petty officers in disbelief then one of them came over and confirmed that it was indeed the truly magnificent *Queen Mary*. I doubt if anyone on board knew the real purpose of the *Keppel's* mission prior to the rendezvous. With so much at stake it had to be 'Top Secret'.

Our prime task had been to escort the cruiser, with her in turn escorting the *Queen Mary* and the speed at which they both travelled meant that our little destroyer's engines really were operating at full speed.

The sight of waves so huge that they actually swamped the bow and foredeck of this long, elegant ocean liner was quite disturbing and, before long, I succumbed to a dreadful bout of sea sickness. Two of the PO's hoisted me up onto the deck. Then, making sure I was fully clothed in my fur lined leather Irvine jacket and trousers (which I still possess) they ultimately lashed me to the upright of a Bofors gun, where I stayed for the rest of the day and the following night. At worst I was semi-conscious, at best I stopped being sea sick. One of my two saviours turned out to be the PO who had been so verbally violent during the torpedo exercise. (There must be a moral in that somewhere.)

Whilst I was oblivious to the events that followed, I was told later that, after a while, the *Queen Mary* and the cruiser continued alone and we slowed down and returned to our Londonderry base.

Later, the cruiser withdrew, the *Queen Mary* went over to full throttle and raced across the mid-Atlantic so fast that no U-boat could even begin to think about attacking her. At the end of her mid-ocean dash she was to be met by a Canadian cruiser and escorted to port.

We finally berthed at Londonderry on the evening of the 24th. I was then transported by road to RAF Eglinton where Plt Off Aseltine was waiting in Hudson T9444, to pilot me on the thirty minute return flight to Aldergrove.

In my subsequent report I emphasised that, in my opinion, there was no future need for Aircrew to liaise in this way with the Navy, as all of us flying operationally over the Atlantic fully understood and sympathised with the Navy's role and their extreme difficulties. The Navy similarly seemed to recognise the RAF's problems and not a single member of the *Keppel's* crew expressed the slightest desire to fly with us. They appeared to prefer a solid deck beneath their feet!

I never heard any more about the need for further 'hands on' close liaison and although I would not have missed this unique experience, it was a great relief to return to the perceived safety of an aeroplane.

Chapter 7
Operations Benbecula

T he 30th June 1942 heralded the beginning of the longest period I was to spend on any RAF Station to date, fourteen months that will remain with me forever. It proved to be an unforgettable experience, not only the exhilaration of being airborne for so much of the time in the quite graceful looking Flying Fortress but also my general participation in life on the remote Outer Hebridean island of Benbecula. My wife Ona and I returned there in 1997 and again in 1999 and the 'magic' of the island remained as potent as it was all those many years ago. Benbecula had an almost overwhelming effect on me, which has only marginally diminished through the passage of time.

The following précis of a quite lengthy war-time article on Benbecula by an unknown author captures the mood and paints a fairly accurate picture; I could readily return there year upon year.

A wryly humorous account of a flight to an Outer Hebrides Coastal Command station

I cannot remember the first time I heard the sinister phrase 'You will be posted to the Outer Hebrides!' Flight Sergeants liked to use it to galvanise non weight-pulling airmen into activity. It seldom failed to have the desired effect. During my time in the ranks, the fear of this posting was ever present. Even when I obtained a Commission and the yellow walls of Air Ministry closed about me, I would stiffen and look nervously to my right and left when the place was mentioned. Then, one day it was suggested that I should visit the Western Isles. I was told that I would travel to a North Country town by train and then fly to the Western Isles by bomber.

The bleakness of Benbecula is evident in this view in early 1941 of the airfield still under construction

I had never flown before. While in the train, I pondered for several hours on the subject of flying. The more I thought about it, the less I liked the immediate outlook. 'P' was waiting for me at the terminus. He was the PRO who was to accompany me on the trip to the Western Isles. He greeted me breezily."You're going to enjoy this trip" he said, "You'll see some of the finest scenery in Scotland. It's terrific!" At the aerodrome we found a wing commander, four sergeant pilots and a large aircraft.

Three of the sergeant Pilots disappeared into the nose and the fourth hid in the tail. There was apparently nowhere for us to sit except on the floor, which was sprinkled with oil and sand. I sat on the oil and sand. 'P' sat on a parachute pack. Then we took off. I enjoyed the first two hours immensely. Then, as we flew over some place which must not be named, we ran into a bump.

I began to feel unwell, and the remaining half hour resulted in a tremendous psychological battle between me and my stomach.

The last five minutes were touch and go. In fact, I became completely indifferent. I didn't care if the slipstream took the top of my head off. I thought that, in the circumstances, it might be the best thing that could happen. One of the sergeants reappeared. He asked me to sit in the end of the aircraft as we were landing. If he had asked me to jump out, I would have done so willingly. I crawled into the tail of the machine and squashed myself into the entrance of the rear-gunner's turret. At that moment, we touched down. Someone pulled the door open and a cold blast pushed into the aircraft. My inside drew a deep breath of relief. Slowly and stiffly I climbed out. The full force of a sixty-mile-an-hour gale, loaded with knives and razor blades, swept through me.

'P' beamed on me, "Welcome to the Outer Hebrides", he said. I stared at the wild, bleak desolation which spread out before me. It was engulfed by a squall of rain. I felt that this was indeed the end. "When do we go back?" I asked, turning up my coat collar, "I'm frozen!"

'P' gaped at me, "Why this is summer!" He pointed out emphatically. I thanked him. At least I had something to be grateful for. Winter in this spot must be terribly bracing.

Together we set out for the distant mess. At the door I paused and looked back at the camp, spread out against the grey sky and rain mists that drifted across the green and brown landscape. The scene was bleak, desolate and wild. The wind, coming in from the Atlantic, found no obstructions to break up its force. Hangars, low wooden buildings and camouflaged Nissen huts built up a picture which depressed me.

We went into the Mess, which was deserted. It was a low wooden affair, somewhat draughty and definitely cold. However, the service was remarkably efficient. A plate of ham and eggs was set before me. My morale soared. 'P' noticed my approval and said, "You've got to go a long way to beat the food on this station. You'll get a tremendous appetite after being here for a day or so. Everyone loves it." At first, I couldn't understand why, but after a while, I found it grew on me. "I've known blokes do their damnedest to stay on when their time's up."

I looked out of the rain-swept window at the scattered buildings and the mud. My spirits declined like a cold soufflé. I said, "Where are we sleeping?"

"It's just down the road," 'P' said, opening the Mess door and letting the gale in.

We stepped into the gale and rain. A quarter of a mile away, some twenty Nissen huts were dotted about the landscape. "Do the officers sleep in, er, these things?" I asked, staring in awe. "Rather" 'P', said lightly. "You'll find them lots of fun."

We entered one of the huts. I regarded the field washing set, the drain pipe stove (unlit) and the grim looking bed with misgivings. The hut was as comfortable and as hospitable as a Nazi concentration camp. I dumped my bag on the bed. "This" I said bitterly, "is the end."

A Nissen hut is made of corrugated iron with wooden window frames and a wooden door let in somehow or other. It is shaped like a barrel which has been split on two. The corrugated iron walls acted as a sounding board. The noise of the wind as it wailed round the hut made me think of 'Wuthering Heights'. I sat on a bed and yawned.

"Do you think," I ventured, "that it would be a bad thing if we summoned a batman and got a fire going?"

"Batman?" 'P' repeated. "They don't have batmen on this station, old boy. Everyone mucks in."

"You mean there'll be no cup of tea in the morning. No buttons polished and perhaps no hot water?" I felt I might just as well know the worst.

"No tea, no polished buttons and certainly no hot water," 'P' returned cheerfully, climbing into bed, "after all this is the Outer Hebrides."

A knock sounded on the door and the Station Adjutant looked in.

"There you are", he said, closing the door, "nippy in here; we'll get a fire going." Here was a man after my own heart. He took a box of matches from his pocket, opened the stove and tossed the lighted match in. The stove began to roar like a ship's furnace. "I'll be right back," he said. "That'll be a decent fire very soon."

When he returned, he carried several tins and three mugs.

"Now we'll have some cocoa and a talk" he said, sitting in the easy chair opposite me. "Reach me the water jug, will you, please?" Silently, I passed it over and he half filled an empty tin which he set on the stove. Then he began to mix the cocoa and condensed milk in the mugs. While he did so, he talked. It was good talk. The warmth from the stove filled the hut. The sound of the wind took on a friendlier note. I suddenly felt differently about

Culla Bay, Benbecula and the author in 'civvies' aged 19 with a very large fossil in July 1942

'The Empire's Last Outpost!' The author standing outside of the Operational Air Crews quarters on Benbecula

this place. Listening to the Adjutant, seeing 'P' lolling back on his elbow in bed, watching the flickering shadows thrown by the paraffin lamp and listening to the roar of the wind, produced an atmosphere which caught my imagination. It was a pleasant, friendly, male atmosphere.

"I have only just arrived" I said. "The place looks grim. I suppose you hate it." The Adjutant's eyes opened.

"When I come to London," he said, "I look around at the crowded streets. I try to see the horizon, but the buildings obstruct my view. I sniff petrol fumes and shudder at the queues forming for buses. I scramble back to the Hebrides as fast as I can. This isle is one of the grandest spots in the world. You can get out on the moors and you can look out across the Atlantic and there's nothing between you and the American coastline. This is a happy station. We are living like men, not like cucumbers in a glasshouse. If you were here any length of time, you'd think the same, unless you have no blood in your veins."

Now to the facts; contrary to expectations, the 30th June transit flight was not to be my last one in a squadron Hudson. On the contrary, we continued with them right up to the end of July and, in the event, were involved in three more operational flights and seventeen others. Each one of the ops flights was an Anti-sub Sweep, the first one in such appalling weather conditions that we were only airborne for three and three quarter hours.

We also fitted in a week of intensive training at the Armament Practice Camp, set up at our old station, Aldergrove. Our training included Shallow Dive Bombing (sixteen bombs), Straight and Level Bombing at 600 feet (again sixteen bombs) plus two lots of Periscope bombing (each of sixteen bombs).

We then moved on to Air/Ground firing, Front, Side (100 rounds) and Rear (200 rounds), repeated again in the afternoon flight.

The following day comprised Air to Air firing - Side and Rear guns with a repeat performance in the afternoon.

We were also involved in quite a number of inter airfield flights on the 17th to Ayr and then from Ayr to Aldergrove for the GAPS Course. After this, we flew to Ballykelly on a return flight, making a similar return trip two days later. We then took in Nutts Corner on the 28th as well as Ballykelly for the third time. Why? I just cannot remember. We stayed overnight and flew back from there to Benbecula on the 29th July.

From then until the 19th August, it was mainly classroom time, being introduced to and learning all about the Flying Fortress and its equipment. It was a major step up from flying in twin engined aircraft to large four engined Fortresses.

Doubtless the pilots were spending a lot of time on circuits and bumps to become thoroughly used to take offs and landings both day and night in these new aeroplanes and at different airfields.

My new skipper was Stan Weir, a flight sergeant at the time, who was promoted to warrant officer at the end of September. We had a variety of co-pilots to begin with, including Alan, but finally settled down with Sgt Parkinson.

On the 1st August, my own promotion to flight sergeant came through along with the accompanying rise in my daily rate of pay to 10/6d. (Just over 50p).

It was the 19th August before I first flew in a Boeing B-17E, FK208(B), with Flt Sgt Clarke as Captain and Stan Weir as co-pilot. We spent an hour and three quarters flying back down to Ireland, Nutts Corner, and two and a half hours on a return trip, Navigation exercise.

The following day was a similar exercise to Burtonwood (two hours, thirty five minutes), returning on the 21st after an overnight stay (two hours, twenty minutes).

On the 23rd, some local flying was intended but we returned to base after fifteen minutes. Guess we developed a fault somewhere. We were airborne again a couple of hours later for Mid-Upper Turret manipulation and beam gun firing. This was powerful fun for a young teenager!

The next three flights were with the Weir/Marriott team in control, averaging two and three quarter hours. D/F Calibration at four points and Turret Manipulation on the first. A Navigation exercise via St. Kilda, Tory Island and Benbecula, again with D/F Calibration, on the second, and an Astro Navigation exercise on the third.

That brought us to the end of our conversion training in August but the new month heralded even more, including Navigation exercises to Prestwick and return on the 5th and a similar return flight on the 9th, to Ballykelly in Northern Ireland with our new commanding officer, Jim Romanes, DFC, as Captain. The co-pilot was Plt Off De la Rue who was sadly killed in a take off accident on the 6th October. For the first time, we were able to do a spot of target shooting using the rear guns. It is a long crawl from the fuselage right down to the tail and when you finally reach the rear gunners position you find yourself on your knees, bent over the cannon, with little room to manoeuvre. Extricating yourself is doubly difficult!

Finally, on the 20th, a penultimate training flight before action; a two and a half hour Night Navigation exercise, taking off at fifty minutes after midnight, Innishtrahull, Tory Island, Benbecula.

Then, on the 24th, five weeks after my initial Fortress flight, we were at last on our very first operation; a nine hour Anti-Sub escort to Convoy UR42. Whilst en route we spotted a naval force; never did find out its purpose.

For some inexplicable reason leave beckoned again and I was away from the 28th September to the 14th October; this was followed by seven consecutive 'ops' flights between the 20th October and the 7th November, ranging from just over eight hours to over eleven hours. The furthest West that we flew was out to 25 degrees and the furthest North to sixty two degrees.

They were mainly Anti-Sub sweeps, although we did link up with Convoys ON143, ONS142, KMF2 and 5C106 on the 3rd November. That surely was a record breaking experience, a series of major events. On the 7th we were protecting Convoy SC107.

Aftermath of the gales at Benbecula 13th December 1942

On two of the October sorties we enjoyed some tangible success. On the 28th in FL457 (F) with the Weir/Parkinson team at the controls, we sighted a U-boat periscope but, by the time we reached the spot where it had submerged, our skipper felt that we were fractionally too late to attack successfully.

Not to be outdone, we were airborne again on the 31st, in roughly the same area, when we sighted another U-boat and this time we were able to attack, dropping six depth charges. We neither forced her to the surface nor saw any wreckage, so I guess she escaped on this occasion.

Sighting a U-boat was one of the most exhilarating experiences anyone of us could wish for. Countless hours, week in - week out, searching the surface of the sea, desperately hoping to spot that black speck indicating a periscope or conning tower, or better still, a thin black streak indicating she was on the surface.

On this occasion, our training and discipline 'Kicked in'. Once the yell over the intercom shouting 'There's a U-boat at 11 o'clock - port side, nearly dead ahead' was received, no one replied 'Where?' everyone just knew instantly what to do and where to station themselves. The pilots and navigators preparing for the attack, bomb doors open, position and course established, radio operator ready to send a 'sighting' message, one beam gunner ready with the camera and the other gunners at their stations; all happening within seconds. No rush, no panic, just moving into top gear as training had dictated.

We stayed in the area for an hour or more in case she had been damaged and had to re-surface, but not this time; a massive anti-climax.

Earlier in the same month, on the 27th, Plt Off Cowey was at 22 degrees West and 59 degrees North when he found U-627 on the surface in 'our' FL457 (F) and sank it with seven depth charges. The luck of the draw!

November was a busy month and, following the ops on the 3rd and 7th, already mentioned, we were out with Convoy ONS144 on the 12th on a Creeping Line Ahead search for a

Boeing Fortress II of 206 Squadron on patrol over The Atlantic from Benbecula. via John Lowe

previously sighted U-boat. On the 17th, we sighted a raft which sadly carried no survivors. On the 26th, we made our longest flight of twelve hours and five minutes and flew further west than ever before, to 28 degrees.

We were on an Anti-sub Sweep around Convoy SC109 and, this time, the 'raft' we sighted carried a Lockheed Lightning. Guess it was the wooden framework that it was lashed to for ease of loading and off loading by crane. There was no sign of the ship that it had been aboard. One can only assume it had been sunk.

On the 30th, out again to 26 degrees West and 54 degrees North on the usual Anti-sub Sweep, this time only ten hours twenty minutes; my fiftieth ops flight.

The final month of the year was very eventful for most of Benbecula. For us it comprised, on the 3rd, a Sweep covering Convoys RU51 and UR 52 up at 61 degrees North, with UR52 on a 300 degree course at eight knots. Then, on the 6th, a CLA search, again at 61 degrees North. We were only out for eight hours, being recalled because of bad weather at base.

On the 8th we flew as a crew to Burtonwood in Lancashire where the American Air Force had a major repair base for Fortresses. I can't remember if we stayed there while AN520 (X) was overhauled, or whether we left it there for routine servicing and enjoyed a few days leave.

We flew back to a traumatised airfield on the 14th. On the previous day, Benbecula had been hit by ferocious gales with near record gusts of 115 mph. The damage to aircraft and hangers was immense and at the height of the storm, ground crews worked unceasingly to avoid aeroplanes being blown over. They could not prevent hangar doors being blown in on top of aircraft though. I did have some cuttings from the many newswpaper reports but they seem to have been mislaid. (If any are reprinted after all you will know I made a more successful repeat search of the loft!) Normally, weather comments were strictly censored, but not this quite extra ordinary event. Within days, the airfield was fully operational and, on the 18th, an eleven hour CLA search covering Convoys RU53 and UR54 took us right up to 62 degrees North, a bit further and we would have sighted Iceland. We also located three isolated MV's and three EV's.

Our final 'op' of 1942 was on the 21st, an eight hour plus Anti-sub Sweep. Before embarking on the hugely busy early months of 1943, it is time to draw breath and consider some of the 'happenings' away from the Battle of the Atlantic. About life on Benbecula itself, in the Sergeants Mess and not least in our Nissen Hut!

Let us begin with our diet. Two quite separate types of food were prepared for us, the very tasty and filling. Aircrew breakfast, served up before take-off on every ops flight, regardless of the time of the day or night. We invariably flew out of Benbecula with full stomachs and the meal always included a fried egg, a luxury for the entire population of the UK, but there were always just enough eggs for us to have one each before ops. Plus, of course, luxury indeed, fried bacon, as well as all the other usuals making up the 'Full English' breakfast.

For the trip, huge Thermos flasks with, I think, three separate containers in each. Inside would be hot mashed potato, meat, probably soup and, if we were VERY lucky, maybe even some green vegetables; sufficient in total to keep seven hungry young aircrew well satisfied; plus, of course, additional Thermos containers of tea or coffee.

The possible vegetable inclusion is stressed as this was a downside to life on the island. All supplies had to come from Scotland on MacBrayne's Steamers and then be transported many, many miles from Loch Boisdale on South Uist. Imagine the tonnages of fuel, of

Schooner mid Atlantic taken from Fortress FL951 28th January 1943 from 800ft above the waves

armaments, depth charges, ammunition etc; of building materials, replacement linen, NAAFI supplies and so very many gallons of beer. And last, but not least, FOOD for the entire station complement. It was not all the food we needed. All too often, apart from potatoes, bulky vegetables were low on the priorities list. We missed green vegetables in our diet and the health of many was, as a result, below standard. Skin problems were of particular concern.

The return journey to and from Loch Boisdale was most unpleasant; a very bumpy road with more than its fair share of pot holes. Our long suffering M.T. (motor transport) drivers did the trip several times a week. Not only for supplies but for taking personnel to or collecting them from the MacBrayne Steamer which would be about to transport them on the first stage of their journey home on leave or from which they would just have disembarked.

I did the return trip twice before asking to see our C.O. Wg Cdr Jim Romanes DFC and describing them in detail. I explained to him that his air crew were supposed to have ten days leave every six weeks, operations permitting. In the event, we travelled by road to Loch Boisdale on Day One, imbibed a few drinks in the local hotel, drinking out of jam jars with string around the neck which, in turn, were secured to a rail around the bar counter, and then boarded the ferry. There were usually sheep on board as well and the conditions were

Above; Boeing Fortress IIA FK190 of 206 Squadron on patrol above the North Atlantic.(Brian Yates via John Lowe).
Below; Another 206 squadron aircraft, this time Fortress IIA FA704 which ditched after attacking and sinking U-417 in the North Atlantic, at 6340N:1100W, approximately 450 miles NNW of Benbecula on the 11th June 1943.
(Maurice McIlwrick via John Lowe)

not even basic. The long sea journey to Oban took many, many hours and the sea was, more often than not, really rough.

Sea sickness was prevalent, particularly among those who had partaken too freely of Boisdale Beer, or eaten a couple of oranges! Should you locate Oban on the map you will soon be aware of the long, tortuous rail journey needed even to reach Glasgow! Remember the black out? The carriages were in virtual darkness, uncomfortable, smelly and with little ventilation. By virtue of the huge distance one had to travel to Southampton, the journey seemed interminable and there were so many stops; worst of all the unscheduled ones when an Air Raid warning sounded.

The memory of peering, bleary eyed out of a steamed up window in an endeavour to read the name of the station you were passing through, remains quite vivid. You tried to play cards, but soon tired of it. If you reached home in the South within two days, you counted yourself lucky.

Just as bad, even worse in fact, was the journey from Mallaig, reached in the summer months from Loch Boisdale via Barra, the island to the South of the Uists. For the return journey, you allowed two and a half days. The rail journey today from Mallaig to Fort William is reported to be one of the most scenically beautiful in the British Isles. In the middle of the war it was a nightmare.

So when I saw the C.O. I explained; two days minimum travelling, one and a half days recovering, four days leave and two and a half days for the return. It made abundant sense to him and he realised his aircrew would not be fit for operations for at least a day, maybe even two, after the return journey from a period of leave. From then on, crews were flown over to the mainland to Thornaby or Burtonwood in the main, with a returning crew flying the aircraft back to Benbecula.

For the outdoor types there was much to do in one's spare time, with so many Lochs full of fish and so many hills to climb. For us less active types, there was the chance to walk out to one of the crofts, meet the motherly lady who was usually the sole occupant and possibly trade some chocolate for eggs or butter which was so rich it could really upset your tummy.

The crofts were just as they had been for centuries (they call them Black Houses nowadays). They consisted of one main low roofed area with a constantly burning peat fire at the end. There were hardly any men folk to be seen. I think the percentage of the male population of the Hebrides who were on active service, predominantly in the Merchant and Royal Navies, was the highest in Western Europe. As a result, the women were fiercely independent. I regret that I did not spend more time visiting the crofters, there was a lot to be learnt from them.

Nowadays, the vast majority of the crofts are in disrepair but close by a 'White' house has been built. A government sponsored scheme to re-house all the crofters. Alongside most of these newish homes stands the inevitable stack of peat, the main source of fuel and, not too far away, will be a flock of sheep.

Thinking of sheep reminds me of lambing time; the island had suffered some ferocious gales about then and, one morning, walking from our Nissen Hut home down to the Sergeants Mess, I came across no less than three dead pregnant ewes in a ditch with the lamb either dead alongside or not quite fully born. Life in the raw, but that was typical of Benbecula.

Now to our 1943 activities, if there seems to be a longish gap between some ops flights it is almost certainly due to the weather, or a leave period, but mainly due to the quite dreadful North Atlantic weather conditions in the winter months.

January saw us airborne on the 13th, 14th, 20th, 23rd and the 28th so there must have been a break in the weather. On the first one, protecting convoy UR58, it really was amazing to realise how very slowly the ships were steaming; five knots on a course of 303 degrees. Apart from the convoy, we also located a couple of Trawlers and of all things a 'Ditched' Barrage Balloon.

The following day, the 14th, we were on stand-by, called 'STRIKE', and ready to take off almost immediately if a sighting report came in. One did, and at 1655 hrs, we were airborne to give extra protection to ONS160 as more than the one U-boat was known to be in the vicinity.

There were twenty six merchant vessels (MVs) in the convoy, escorted by five naval vessels, (EV's).We were out for nine and a half hours, returning at about 0200 hrs. Our second replacement, Plt Off Clark, captaining FL452 (G), the aircraft we had ourselves flown in, left Benbecula at 0733 and at 1445 hrs, whilst shadowing ONS160, sighted U-632 on the surface and dropped four depth charges, causing some damage. As I said earlier, the luck of the draw!

By now, Stan Weir's commission had come through and since the beginning of the year he had become Plt Off Weir.

The Creeping Line Ahead search on the 20th was uneventful and we were only able to stay out there for eight and three quarter hours as the conditions were far too rough. We managed ten hours on the 23rd with Convoy UR58 and, during our searches in it's vicinity, we located two trawlers and then six scattered MVs in a line ahead 1 - 3 - 1 - 1. We pointed them towards the comparative safety of UR58.

There was another ten hour trip on the 28th, taking care of Convoy UR60. In our searches we came across three MVs and one escort vessel, all scattered. Later on, we encountered three more MVs and an escort vessel to the Port side and, much later, an MV seven miles ahead. For good measure, we also sighted a three masted Icelandic Schooner RE150.

If ever one single ops flight encapsulated the war in the North Atlantic, this was it. One could imagine the horrors these scattered MVs and EVs witnessed and I imagine that the sight of a friendly UK aircraft might have lifted their morale a little. On the other hand, they probably thought 'Those lucky b's will be back on dry land in a few hours, and we are out here for many more dangerous days.' Our merchant seamen had as rough a deal as almost any serviceman, along with the navy types.

February was equally busy with seven ops flights ranging from a mere six and three quarter hours up to eleven hours. Then an Anti-sub Sweep on the 1st, take off 0445 and a W/T homing onto a damaged sloop- on the 5th and the provision of 'close escort.'

Then, on the 8th, came another W/T homing, this time onto Convoy SC118 and again we had to provide close escort. These were dangerous times for all vessels on the Atlantic and it was no surprise that, on the following day, Sqn Ldr Patrick in FK195(L), the Fortress we flew in on the 5th, found U-614 on the surface at 1242 hours and the depth charges dropped caused damage. For the third time, the luck of the draw!

On the 16th, our CLA search for a known U-boat in the area did not meet with the same success. The following day we enjoyed a training break with plenty of air firing and low level bombing.

Back on ops at 7 o'clock the next morning; (think how early we were turfed out of our bleak Nissen Huts and trundled down to the Mess for our Air Crew Breakfast), followed by a briefing session in the Ops Room. I swore then that I would never take a job in Civvy Street that involved getting up in the middle of the night and having to be on duty at dawn, this being the time we were usually well on our way across the Atlantic.

By now, SC119 was in our area and we again carried out a series of Anti-sub Sweeps around her.On one we found a lonely MV, quite small, and directed her to the convoy.

Two days later, on an eleven hour flight, we were out protecting HX226, yet another convoy. There were so many of them but each one was different. Different in course and speed, different in the types of Merchant ships involved, different in the number of close escort Naval vessels and the size of them. But most of all different in their overall shape and size, depending on whether you were seeing them complete, not long after sailing, or whether you were seeing them two thirds of the way across the Atlantic after several U-boat attacks.

You make a head count as soon as possible after first contact and, all too often, the number proves to be less than the number the Ops Room had told you to expect. Nearly every day was a sad day and your heart filled with sympathy for those in the ships below. We hardly ever located any survivors from the attacks. 'Tis a huge, huge ocean and a life raft is so tiny in context. Nowadays, our Nimrods would have no difficulty in locating them, but, with Radar in its infancy, we had no such success.

The weather closed in and we were diverted to Aldergrove. It was two days before we could fly back to Benbecula and even then it took nearly an hour and a half.

ONS169 was our next convoy on the 27th. On the 14th January, we had been out with ONS160 which meant that in just six weeks we covered nearly ten convoys on the ONS route alone, slow Outward Bound to Nova Scotia, having been looked after by a Coastal Command squadron, mainly 206, as well as the UR, and RUs, the SC and HX's together with ON's and countless others.

This 'op' on the 27th was a fairly straight-forward Anti-sub Sweep of nine and a half hours up to nearly 60 degrees North.

There was no let up in March and, as a whole, it was one of the squadron's best months with three U-boats being sunk by Fortress depth charge attacks; one on the 19th, near to HX229, U-384, by Plt Off Clark, the second on the 25th, near convoy RU67, U-469, by Flt Lt Roxburgh and the third on the 27th whilst on a CLA search, U-169, by Fg Off Samuel.

You'll not believe this, but I really did fly over to the mainland on the 18th and was away for the rest of March on leave! Consequently, I missed all three sinkings. Fortunately I returned in time for more success in April. These were indeed 'heady' days.

But to revert to early March and the five ops trips that I did manage to be on duty for; these were some of the saddest days, with exceptional convoy losses, combined with appalling weather conditions in the middle of the month. A U-boat hunt on the 1st, only seven hours as weather forced us back and into a landing at Skitten on the Scottish mainland. This Op saw me reaching my five hundredth ops hour. The return flight next day took an hour and a half.

Up long before dawn on the 3rd to act as escort to HX227, fifty six MVs, six EVs and one MV straggler; airborne ten and a quarter hours. The 7th saw us looking after ON170 and ONS171, fifty two MVs and five EVs in ON170 alone in almost continuous snow and sleet. We had no option but to return early after nine and three quarter hours of horrendous turbulence.

Then, on the 13th and the 14th came the two most poignant operational flights of my RAF career. Again in appalling weather conditions out to 28 degrees West on thefirst flight searching for survivors and wrecks from the so very badly damaged convoy SC121, repeated the following day out to 27 degrees West. We were airborne for ten and three quarter hours and eleven hours respectively, in each case taking off just after 0500 hrs.

To fly out West, looking for seamen and wrecks, using a creeping line ahead pattern, was a heartbreaking task; knowing in your heart that the chances of anyone surviving in almost freezing temperatures and mountainous seas was very remote. Oh yes! There was plenty of debris and you had to fly low over it and investigate, just in case, but it really was a distressingly hopeless task.

I think those two days had a more sobering effect on the squadron than anything else we had experienced. It was a relief when we went on leave on the 18th, even though we missed the U-boat sinkings on the 19th, 25th and 27th March previously detailed; three sinking's in eight days. Perhaps it was poetic justice after the horrors of the earlier SC121 losses.

There was still much to come on our return and April was indeed a good month for the squadron and for our own crew as well.

But before all this, what else was happening on the island? In the MT section, we enjoyed the presence of Tom Blue, a great character. Ona and I met up with him on 206 Squadron re-unions, particularly the ones at Benbecula, and we re-lived the early 1940's. He told us many stories of the MTs various adventures, both on the airfield, collecting aircrew from their Nissen huts in the middle of the night, meeting the returning aircrew after their flights and, at the airfield, primarily on the Benbecula/Loch Boisdale and return journeys.

Perhaps his best story concerned the S.S. *Politician*, the ship which ran aground in the South of the islands, loaded with whisky! Remember the film 'Whisky Galore'? It was based on the wrecking of the *Politician*.

Huge numbers of cases were rescued from the wreck by the islanders and the MT section got involved, helping to distribute them before the 'Revenue' arrived. Quite a few found their way onto the airfield, many of which were hastily buried out there. It is said that none could be retrieved before a concrete runway was laid over their hiding places. I wonder what future generations will make of it if ever the runway were to be lifted and an archaeologist moved in with his metal detector, or maybe even a water diviner located them! I miss Tom Blue. He was a good man.

In the kinder summer months, we paid an occasional visit to Culla Bay, a nearby stretch of beautiful silver sand. Wearing civilian clothes was not frowned upon in those days and I have a picture of me at Culla Bay in 'civvies'. These must have come off on our visit to enable us to sun-bathe. I doubt if we swam in those icy Atlantic waters! I know we did the former because we finished up at the medical officer's Surgery with sunburn and prickly heat, only to be told that a self inflicted wound was a Court Martial offence! We spent ages lying on our wet canvas camp beds, getting up periodically to pour cold water over our fellow sufferers. I would guess that, after a long winter on the island, without exposing our bodies to the air, let alone sunshine and, being deprived of adequate vegetables, our skins were probably lily white and ultra sensitive to the sun's rays. At least it has served as a warning not to repeat the incident over the sixty plus ensuing years!

(xv.)

```
           Fortress D/206
           Captain - P/O Weir
           2203 - 22nd April, 1943
           62.57N  12.15W
           S.E. of Iceland

           Aircraft on A/S patrol at 1,200 feet, sighted conning tower
of 'U' Boat which was surfacing five to six miles distant on
starboard beam, and attacked along track of 'U' Boat from
astern, releasing six 250 lb Torpex depth charges, set at 25
feet, spaced at 100 feet, from a height of 80 feet, 22 seconds
after conning tower had disappeared.    Centre of stick fell
just forward of swirl, up track of 'U' Boat.    Aircraft remained
in the vicinity for 13 minutes, nothing further was observed,
and aircraft left to carry out baiting procedure.
```

Wish I had secured
the reports of other
Moments in my career
with 206 T.

/ (xvi) ....

Then there were the indoor activities. When, not flying, we spent time in the crew room with training lecturers and identification classes. The latter were so intense that I am sure we were able to identify the silhouette of every known Allied and German aeroplane, and certainly every Naval vessel.

During off duty time we played cards a great deal, with quite large schools of Pontoon in particular.Games like Bridge and Whist never really 'took off' but Pontoon and, to a much lesser degree, Poker, were the most popular. The Pontoon sessions were usually supported by the same crowd and I doubt if any of us 'won' or 'lost' to any degree.

We did have one fellow who 'let the side down' though.He had enjoyed a winning streak and some one saw him in our tiny village Post Office putting a few pounds into a PO Savings Account. A few days later he was in a 'School', lost a pound or so, and declared he had to 'quit' as he had 'run out' of cash. The next day he won and on this occasion he walked away from the game and was later seen depositing his winnings in the Post Office again. Another day, another 'School' and he lost a little, once more said he had 'run out' of cash and exited the game.

The next occasion that we played saw all of us close together around the table and when he arrived he was unable to find a space to put his chair. No-one commented, we just stayed bunched together and slowly he sat down on the fringe and watched. He was never able to join any gambling card school again and it was not really discussed; just a spontaneous act by lads who felt that he had 'crossed the line' by not allowing us the chance to win back any of our losses. We just ensured that he could not salt away any more of our meagre pay.

Another indoor event was a 'dance'. Whether we held more than one in the Sergeants Mess I cannot remember, but it fell to Tom Blue and his trusty MT drivers to call at all the local crofts and further afield, to collect all the ladies who had been previously notified of 'The Dance' to the Mess.

They were indeed Bonnie Lassies who showed no mercy, whether it was an Eightsome Reel or a Fox Trot. They were so fit and so strong, we were like straw dolls in their hands. I know I was exhausted after about three dances! They really were charming and delightful guests but they certainly made most of us feel like weaklings.

You are bound to wonder, bearing in mind our proximity to the islands of Lewis and Harris, just to the North, whether any Harris Tweed came our way. Indeed it did, woven on our 'own' island, but not fully 'aired'.

I purchased a length of blue, which we had made into a long outdoor coat for my mother, another length for a long brown coat for me and a browny/white quantity for a sports coat. Snag was that they always had an 'aroma' about them, a very kind word in the event!

Now back to business and the successful month of April, starting on the 10th with a ten and a half hour Anti-sub Sweep covering convoys ON177 and ONS3, we also sighted SC125. Take off time 0615 hrs.

On the 16th another ten and a half hour op, this time carrying out a CLA ahead of Convoy RU70. Take off time 0415, so guess we were turned out of our beds before 2 am!

Then, at last, on the 22nd, right up at 63 degrees North and on a CLA for a previously sighted U-boat, we spotted her coming to the surface. We all moved into top gear for the bombing run and optimistically dropped six of our depth charges. We were certain that we had straddled her as she submerged but were shattered when she failed to re-appear or even soil the water with an oil streak. In the event we decided that she had sunk to the bottom. Sadly, post war enquiries into German Naval records revealed that she was able to return to base. Still, this was our third sighting of a German U-boat and our second attack. With hindsight we felt we had 'done our bit'.

On the 28th we were on STRIKE stand by when word came in of a Bristol Beaufort ditching into the sea off Barra Head leaving the crew in a dinghy. We were airborne within minutes at 1255 hrs and, although we searched for four hours before being recalled, we failed to locate them. The next day we did some practice low level bombing with sixteen releases.

Earlier, on the 24th, two days after our own attack, Plt Off Cowey sighted and attacked U-710 at 61 degrees north before she could submerge. Despite this attack, she remained on the surface so he came round for a second attack and this time she was sunk in the vicinity of convoy ONS5.

May 1943 began with an 0525 take off on the 1st when we were charged with looking after Convoys SC127 and ONS6, the former comprising thirty four MVs and just three escorts. We performed our usual Anti-sub Sweep all around each one in turn but no U-boat appeared. They were already being much more wary when aircraft were aloft.

On the 5th, I had my first and only flight in Fokker F.XXII, HM159, piloted by Sqn Ldr Hankin; a transit flight to Port Ellen and then on to Abbotsinch, a total of nearly two hours. Need I say it? Going on leave again!

By the time of my return, I had left my teenage years behind me, having celebrated my 20th birthday on the 15th, then found myself re-crewed with a Sgt Dyer as pilot, with Fg Off Chisholme as co-pilot, probably due to my seniority, as they were both relatively new. Leaving Stan Weir was a wrench but he was coming to the end of his tour of duty in any case. I stayed with the Dyer/Chisholme team until my own tour came to an end in August.

Initially there were hours of circuits and bumps, firstly Check Solos then Solos, followed then by nearly five hours of Night Duals and Solos. I can hardly bear to think about it now, taking off and landing, time and time again in a strange (very strange for the pilot) four engined aircraft at an unfamiliar airfield, both in daylight and for several hours after midnight. I would not undertake such a task now for <u>any</u> financial reward at all. It was potentially suicidal! Yet at the time we never gave it more than a passing thought!

There were then the inevitable Navigation Exercises, firstly to Prestwick, then, after an overnight stay, a near five hour exercise via Rockall to Benbecula. As the end of May approached, we flew up to Stornoway and landed. In the afternoon we flew to and around Galan Head on a photographic exercise, landing again at Stornoway. The evening saw us make the return flight to Benbecula.

Just after midnight on the 30th there were more night take offs and landings carried out more times than I care to remember, and they say nowadays that 'tis only on take off or landing that there is any risk in flying! We were doing them by the dozen with a relatively inexperienced Captain! Then, for good measure, the following night saw us performing this take off and landing routine again, complete with a four hour Night Navigation Exercise.

June started off quite well, there was a final training flight, incorporating local familiarisation flying together with some low level practice bombing, followed on the 4th, by the first operational flight of the new crew, a CLA, Anti-sub patrol. It proved to be my longest ever flight in a Fortress (twelve and a half hours) in excess of the aircraft's maximum duration. In the event, we had to be diverted to Skitten, up near Wick in Caithness in the top North East corner of Scotland. Whether this was because of our fuel situation or because of bad weather in the Outer Hebrides, I cannot remember, but we were able to make the one and a half hour return journey later the next day. Following this, there was more pilot training, mainly low level bombing which was essential if we were to successfully straddle a U-boat.

The month then became busy. On the 10th we were out on a CLA covering convoy UR78 comprising just five MVs and three Trawlers. This was an early 0425 hrs take off, there's no wonder that I now hate early rising! Bad weather forced us back after only seven and a quarter hours and we had to land at Ballykelly in Northern Ireland as Benbecula was at zero visibility. Fortunately, it cleared later on and we were able to make the return flight of one and a half hours to base in the evening.

On the 11th, our relatively new C.O., Wg Cdr Thompson DSO, attacked and sunk U-417 at 64 degrees north, 10 degrees west. The U-boat remained on the surface, however, and kept firing at our aircraft on the bombing run so effectively that it crashed into the sea. Fortunately, all the crew were able to scramble out into the only dinghy, which survived the crash, and, most importantly the Wireless Operator managed to send not only a U-boat sighting report but also a May Day call. The S.O.S. was heard and all squadrons in the North West and the Navy were advised, then a major search operation began, which was not helped by the survivors being in the middle of a minefield.

Our turn came at 1415 hours and we combed the reported area using a square search pattern. For some now unknown reason we returned after only eight and a half hours. We rested on the 12th but took off again at 0200 hrs on the 13th, this time using the CLA search pattern. We were in the area for so long that we had to be diverted to Reyjkavick in Iceland as we would never have made it back to base; even then we had been up for over twelve hours.

We rested on the 14th and took the opportunity to load the aircraft with that almost unobtainable commodity - CHOCOLATE, from the American PBX. Iceland was full of Americans and was also an assembly point for some of the convoys, particularly those on the most hazardous journeys to and from Murmansk in Russia.

Then news arrived of a second 'ditching', this time by a Catalina of 190 Squadron, which had attempted to land near to the recently located Fortress crew, sadly without success. The waves were too high, and swamped it. We therefore set off on the 15th at 1500 hours and began our CLA search, only leaving the area when it became too dark to see anything on the water. On the return journey to Benbecula, we began to lose engine power (the full story on this see Chapter 8). The total airborne time was just over ten hours. The 'powers that be' let us rest a while but 206 Squadron remained busy with Fg Off Clarke damaging U-338 on his second depth charge attack on the 17th.

We resumed operational flying on the 21st with another Anti-Sub Patrol in excess of twelve hours, Anti-Sub Patrol, returning in the early hours of the 22nd. On the 24th we flew down to Langford Lodge in Northern Ireland for another Navigation Exercise, returning the following day. The weather was so bad on our next ops flight on the 27th, an Anti-Sub Sweep, that we had no alternative but to return after only six and three quarter hours. Finally, on the 30th, we spent nearly four hours making mock attacks on a British submarine off the Maidens.

On the 4th July, I was granted my commission and became a pilot officer, although for some reason or another it was not promulgated until I had left the squadron!

On the 5th, we spent ten and three quarter hours on a CLA 'Catspaw' patrol (all sorts of lovely new names were appearing at this time). We located eleven MVs steering 120 degrees at seven knots and later three destroyers steering 315 degrees at fifteen knots.

On the 10th, we practiced BABS for about half an hour. Then, on the 11th, a ten and three quarter hour CLA 'Mooring Four' Patrol when we sighted a solitary MV doing six knots on 310 degrees. This was followed on the 17th by a CLA 'Moorings Two' Patrol of ten and a half hours.

The 20th saw us again practicing BABS for over an hour and finally, on the 21st July 1943, my very last squadron operational flight, lasting over ten and a half hours (the eighty seventh), bringing my total operational flying up to just on seven hundred hours, an average of about eight hours per flight.

I sometimes add in later flights, out to Gibraltar, North Africa and the Azores, as they were in war zones and liable to enemy air attack, so I could claim in excess of ninety operational flights and over seven hundred and thirty ops hours. But it matters not; let's settle for a huge amount of both flights and hours and having miraculously survived them all.

On the 23rd, I was flown over to West Freugh for another spot of leave, returning at the beginning of August. From then on it was a series of training flights including practice bombing and air to sea firing.Then there was a series of inter airfield flights. On the 7th, we went over to Silloth, then down to Speke and finally to Thorney Island. On this trip, I completed my overall flying time of one thousand hours. After an overnight stay we were flying back when we became lost. We decided that our best option was to seek out an airfield, land, and somehow or other find out where we were without letting on that we were truly lost!

Two Fokker F.XXIIs were impressed into military service during October 1941. Both HM159 and HM160 eventually served with 1 AONS at Prestwick, the former crashing into Loch Tarbut on the 3rd July 1943 a mere two months after Ted's flight. HM160 survived the work to serve Scottish Airlines as G-AFZP. via Martyn Chorlton

The airfield turned out to have the quite amazing name of Snitterfield. We landed and taxied fairly close to the Control Tower, realised we were flying an operational Flying Fortress with plenty of fairly secret equipment on board and hastily mounted a guard front and rear as we were besieged by very envious ground staff. A Flying Fortress with RAF roundels was indeed a unique bird. Having found out where we were, we were soon on our way (within a quarter of an hour), we finished up at Hawarden for the night. An early ten minute flight to Speke on the 9th and then a two and a half hour flight back to Benbecula.

On the 11th, Alan, by now a warrant officer, flew me over to Prestwick for more leave. I duly returned and finally, finally was flown out of Benbecula for the very last time the 30th August, in a Fortress of 220 Squadron to Thornaby, my posting flight en-route to the Coastal Command Development Unit at Dale, in the far west of South Wales, called the 'Little England beyond Wales'.

I have never understood the discrepancies between official dates and actuals, my commission being a recent example. Now, here we had my being 'Officially' posted to CCDU on the 12th August but yet not scheduled to arrive there until the 3rd September. That may account for my being sent on leave on the 11th August!

So I came to the end of an era. Fourteen months of unforgettable experiences, of amazing flights out into the North Atlantic, living through some of the most violent weather of the entire war, seeing convoys disintegrating almost day by day, sighting and attacking enemy submarines, standing by as friends and colleagues disappeared. They just failed to return from a flight and were never seen nor heard of again.

Benbecula today. Still an RAF station, changed very little from its Second World War layout. via Martyn Chorlton

Coincidentally, there were many other postings, as the squadron was about to be taken 'out of line', in readiness for its transfer to those remote islands that make up the Azores. Anyone approaching the end of his tour of duty left at this time as the RAF had no wish to send air crew out to this new base if within a month or two they would be due to go 'On Rest'. It really was the end of an era for everyone.

Just for the record, 206 Squadron were scheduled to go to the Azores in August but did not actually arrive there until early October. It was needed there as the bulk of the U-boats were now operating in more Southern Latitudes, the North Atlantic having become too hot for them.

The squadron was only out there for about six months, returning in March and converting on to Liberators in readiness for the massive talk of keeping the English Channel totally free of U-boats and other enemy Naval vessels, during the run up to D-Day on the 6th June 1944 and thereafter.

But, for me, my new life began in earnest on the 4th anniversary of the start of the war, the 3rd September 1943 and is detailed in Chapter Nine.

Chapter 8
Failed to Return

In the case of Coastal Command, all too often over the seas and oceans, not least the North Atlantic, the crew just 'failed to return' from a flight. No detail, no last minute message, no SOS, not a single word of explanation. Not necessarily operational, not necessarily over enemy territory. They just disappeared, but why? And how?

The loss of these highly trained crews and much-needed aircraft added to the appalling loss of life during the Battle of the Atlantic and the almost unsustainable losses of ships and supplies. The losses and the continuous heroic role of the Royal Navy are well-documented, as is the suffering that the crews endured.

The RAF squadrons of Coastal Command flew out over the Atlantic on a daily basis, all too often in appalling weather conditions and FTR, represented a significant proportion of their losses.

During the earlier years of the war, we were not blessed with modern navigational aids, relying almost entirely on 'DR', (Dead Reckoning), an appropriate name under the circumstances.

DR relied on regular estimates of wind speed and direction, mainly by studying our 'drift' relative to the wave white caps and by the use of a sextant. All too often, distractions disturbed the Navigator's efforts to maintain a constant plot, including the sighting of and attacking a U-boat, the sighting of an unexplained vessel, circling a convoy and being diverted to seek out a possible threat or a 'straggler' and not least search for a lifeboat of survivors.

Any miscalculation could lead the Navigator to think, it was still safe to continue the patrol, when he should have been advising the pilot to return to base. Such miscalculations often proved fatal as the resultant shortage of fuel meant ditching in the hostile Atlantic with virtually no hope of rescue or survival. So yet another Coastal Command crew's epitaph became FTR. Having nearly become an FTR casualty on three separate occasions during my eighty seven operational flights I feel qualified to comment.

In June 1942, we were returning from the 1000 Bomber raid on Bremen to a small satellite airfield of North Coates with the exotic name of Donna Nook. We were flying in Lockheed Hudson AM722, as part of 206 Squadron's contribution of twelve aircraft.

In the half light of pre-dawn, the North Sea looks very inhospitable and, having spent quite a while avoiding hostile flak and night fighters, we were not at all sure of our position and were running very low on fuel. In the Operations Room there was real concern as 25% of the squadron's planes had then 'Failed to Return', including the one containing our new commanding officer, Wg Cdr Cooke.

Our Skipper, Fg Off Eric Bland, sighted a smudge on the horizon, the East Coast of Britain and with five pairs of eyes scanning the rapidly approaching land, we were soon able to identify the area and raced to North Coates to find out that we had already been recorded as 'MISSING'. It was recognised that, by then, we should have run out of fuel. In fact, the ground crew confirmed that there were only minutes of flying time remaining in the tanks.

The other two 'Missing' aircraft did 'Fail to Return', having been shot down over target. One of them contained my crew mate and best friend, Joe Peet, who spent the rest of the war in various German POW camps. After the war, at a 206 Squadron reunion, he told the story of how he 'fell out' of his Hudson over the burning city of Bremen and was captured before he could be lynched by some very, very angry survivors of our bombing.

On another occasion, in June 1943, on my eighty first Ops Flight, when searching for the crew of Catalina 'C' of 190 Squadron which had crashed into the Atlantic during an attempt to land and rescue the crew of Fortress 'R' of 206 Squadron that had been shot down whilst attacking and sinking a U-boat, we were returning from an earlier diversion to Iceland in Boeing Fortress FK213(C) piloted by Sgt Dyer.

We began to experience loss of power in a couple of engines and were losing too much height for comfort. The order came to jettison everything that could be moved. Down went the depth charges, the cannon, ammunition, seats were wrenched from their mountings, even the ELSAN, the toilet, had to go.In the end we had to jettison the mountains of chocolate, probably more than existed in the whole of Scotland, that we had secured from the American PBX in Reykjavik for the officers, sergeants and other ranks mess halls in Benbecula in the Outer Hebrides. Finally, with our appearing to approach sea level faster than we were approaching our island home, we just made it, avoiding becoming yet another FTR statistic.

Six operational flights later, I was sent on rest, having survived my first tour of nearly seven hundred operational hours. But it was not only navigational errors or engine problems that resulted in an FTR Situation. Weather and changes in barometric pressure were also to blame. Waves in the Atlantic can be as high as the deck of an ocean liner and, if the barometric pressure had changed significantly and the cloud base was virtually zero, trouble loomed.

All too often, an aircraft descending through dense cloud is theoretically at a safe height based on the altimeter reading, which, in turn, is based on the pressure at base on take off. A significant change can produce a situation where the pilot/navigator thinks the plane is at 100ft when it is actually down to 50ft, then a coincidental 50ft wave then claws the aircraft into the sea. I know it does, I was there in a Fortress piloted by a flight sergeant, nicknamed 'Shortie', when it so very nearly happened to us.

The weather had been so appalling that, one by one, the Wireless Op/Air Gunners succumbed to air sickness and were prostrate on the fuselage floor. For once, I was not so badly affected and crawled along the gangway of the bomb bay to find Stan alone in his cushioned seat with no co-pilot. He was semi-conscious in the nose of the Fortress with the collapsed navigator.

I remember shouting across to the pilot above the roar of the four engines that he had no crew left and, even if we saw one, it would be a million to one chance to attack a sub in such tempestuous seas. I remember shouting again that we ought to climb out of the danger, get above the clouds and go home.

Fortunately, he was just about above exhaustion level and we began to climb. As we did so, the turbulence slowly abated, the crew began to recover and we survived. The memory of the height of those waves is as vivid today as it was sixty five years ago.

Chapter 9
Non-Operational Flying

CCDU Dale and Angle, South Wales

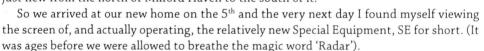

My arrival at the small airfield of Dale, at the South Western point of Wales, early in September 1943, heralded my shortest posting during the entire war. I first set foot on the airfield on the fourth anniversary of the beginning of the war, the 3rd September and just forty eight hours later I was on board Halifax II HR672 (K), piloted by Sqn Ldr John Stone, a flight commander, for the fifteen minute flight to the unit's new base at RAF Angle. We just flew from the north of Milford Haven to the south of it!

So we arrived at our new home on the 5th and the very next day I found myself viewing the screen of, and actually operating, the relatively new Special Equipment, SE for short. (It was ages before we were allowed to breathe the magic word 'Radar').

The headlong rush into the work of the CCDU, was breath taking and I was airborne not only on the 6th but also on the 8th, twice on the 10th, the 11th, 13th, 15th, 16th, twice on the 17th and then on eleven more occasions in the month. All in all, twenty two flights in four different aircraft, three times in a Beaufighter, twice in a Halifax, three times in a Hudson and seven in a Wellington. Consequently, I was on rest with a bump especially having flown with six different pilots, all experienced flight lieutenants plus a squadron leader and a wing commander.

We were trialing new and improved equipment; there were trials with a submarine off Fishguard, dropping new type flares, practicing Leigh Light operations, firing RPs (Rocket Projectiles), it was very exhilarating diving down at high speed, firing them in two bursts and then pulling out of the dive, a definite must for anyone seeking a thrill a second.

The month also included flights to stormy Stoney Down, Harrowbeer, Northolt, Farnborough and Defford and, by its end, I could not help but feel that if this was meant to

CCDU Officers and airmen in September 1943; author is on leave!

be a 'Rest period' the quicker I returned to operational flying the better! Especially when, on the 25th, the rear exit on the Beaufighter VIC JL832 (D), piloted by Flt Lt Blackmore, opened in flight and we had to make an emergency landing at Farnborough.

For some inexplicable reason, bearing in mind that I did not attend a commissioning interview at No.19 Group H.Q. until the 22nd September, my commission was actually backdated to the 4th July; whilst I was still on 206 Squadron. Even stranger, my promotion from flight sergeant to warrant officer was dated 2nd August 1943, after my commissioning date. Then, finally, on the 17th October, I was awarded a Good Conduct badge and an increase of 3d per day in my pay! As a pilot officer, no longer 1181644 but now 159526, I was now on the princely rate of 14/6d per day and had at last passed the 12/6d which had enticed me into the RAF. It had taken just over three years to achieve!

I gradually came to terms with my new life on CCDU and found myself quite enjoying the huge variety of tasks we had to undertake, so much so that, when my Commission finally came through I approached the many ground crew that I had come to know in the short time, I had been in the unit and asked them to be particularly respectful when I donned my officers' uniform and to give me the odd salute.

This was done to impress the C.O. Wg Cdr Anstead AFC, as it was customary for anyone being commissioned to be posted away from their present station on the grounds that it might prove difficult for them to establish their authority over other ranks with whom they had previously socialised.

In the event it semi-backfired! Two days after appearing in my smart new officers' uniform, I had to accost nearly everyone and tell them to 'Stop it!' The word had spread about my request that I receive the odd respectful salute and I am sure that every AC2, AC, LAC, Corporal, Sergeant and Flight Sergeant, both RAF and WAAF flung up a salute of parade ground quality wherever I went. A spot of light relief for all concerned, it took me hours going back around the Station saying 'Stop it. Please!'

I was quite chuffed when I heard that I was not to be posted, until I later discovered that I had been 'headhunted' onto the Unit to act as Sub-Editor of the reports we produced on the outcome of trials. This duty was in addition to being a coordinator of trials, an R/T Operator, a W/T Operator, an SE Operator, etc., etc. I could not have been transferred in any case! This was no sinecure post which had come my way though!

I had better now comment on the many functions of CCDU, which, in itself, is a fairly explicit title, development being at the heart of it. The development of a host of new and improved products for Coastal Command. We covered Anti Ship, Anti-submarine, Navigational and Photography products with an emphasis on Radar.

We carried out test trials onBomb Sights, Night Photography, the NW Gee Chain, Air/ Sea Rescue aids, various Marks of ASV, various types of Navigational Aids, Sea Return Discriminators, Anti Snorkel devices, Rocket Projectiles and even Flares. Each one was in conjunction with the Scientists involved at establishments such as RAE Farnborough.

On the Unit we had our own Scientific Officer, Dr. Pickard, together with his assistant. He was a young man of many talents who seemed to enjoy his day more if he had nearly completed the 'Times' crossword before starting work!

Very quickly all concerned developed the necessary skills needed to be involved with these quite often very complicated products and in the rapid and exhaustive proving of their respective capabilities.

The many processes required a wide range of aircraft, very rarely of front line quality, probably each one being a squadron or training unit 'cast off'.In just over sixteen months at Angle, I flew in no less than ten different aircraft, from an Avro Anson to a Vickers Wellington, as well as in a Sunderland at nearby Pembroke Dock. As for pilots, well, my log books record that I flew with no less than thirty seven different pilots at Angle, more than on any other Station, Squadron or Unit on which I served throughout the war. From Flt Lt Ainsworth, with whom I flew on sixteen occasions in a Beaufighter and in Wellingtons, to Plt Off Williamson, twelve occasions; in an Anson and again in Wellingtons. My most flights were with Flt Lt Houston, thirty one, once in a Proctor and fifteen times each in Halifaxes and Wellingtons.

From this it can be seen that the work-horse Wellington was hugely employed and between December 1941 and March 1946, I made two hundred and eighteen flights in them, even more than in the Hudson and in the Fortress, mainly at Angle but also some at a later Station, Thorney Island.

The 10th December 1941 flight was a 'one off', a journey from Aldergrove to Hawarden (going on leave) piloted by a Captain Chambers of the Air Transport Auxiliary. Well, not quite 'one off', as before Angle I was again transported on leave in a Wellington from Aldergrove to Hawarden by ATA 1st Officer Turnell on the 28th January 1942.

What's this? On leave 10th December and again on the 28th January, only a seven week gap? Well, believe it or not, operations permitting, the 'Powers that be' had decreed that Aircrew needed ten days leave every six weeks!! It very rarely proved possible but once it did! However, that was on an operational squadron, we definitely did not have that much leave with CCDU!

Newly commissioned, July 1943 aged 20

CCDU Officers Mess or 'The Hall' at Angle

Now reverting to the considerable number of different types of aircraft we required for the wide range of trials, imagine the many daily problems faced by our Engineer, Flt Lt Munro. He had built up a highly skilled team of fitters, riggers, wireless and armaments experts, radar technicians and engineers. He had needed to, not for him the luxury of just working on say Hudsons, he had to be 'au fait' with nearly a dozen different types, and mainly 'second hand' aeroplanes into the bargain!

Imagine them all, the Anson, the Beaufighter, a Catalina, Halifax, Hudson, Liberator, Proctor, Ventura, Warwick and Wellington. Plus, of course, an involvement with the Sunderlands at Pembroke Dock! And, as I said earlier, I flew in all of them!

Bearing this in mind, it will not come as a surprise to hear that the pilots on CCDU were largely hand picked. Specialists on one particular type of aircraft included those pilots from Beaufighter and Mosquito squadrons, Hudsons and Wellington and, not least the highly experienced four engine types to fly the Halifax, the Liberator and, later at Thorney Island, the Lancaster. Their experience and well honed skills counter-balanced the age of most of our fleet, as did the skills and experience of the highly professional ground crews.

It was largely due to this combination that, when crises occurred, as they did indeed, not only on take offs and landings, but also when airborne, there was, at the controls, an expert, well able to handle whatever emergency arose.

The several emergencies I was personally involved in, as detailed at the end of this chapter, were all successfully handled by the specialist pilot concerned. I will be forever grateful to them all, I was indeed well 'watched over'. Or I was born under a Lucky Star!

There was a time when a member of the aircrew team felt that he would be in a safer environment if he could terminate his 'Rest period' and revert to squadron operational flying in just one type of aircraft!Such a request fell on deaf ears, not only because of the vital importance of our research and trialing but also because each member of air crew had developed exceptional skills in the rapid, yet exhaustive, proving of the particular equipment sent to us by the 'boffins'.

My move from the Sergeants Mess to the Officers Mess was a major event in the life of this 'young' twenty year old. The dining and rest rooms were on the airfield, which in itself was on high cliffs forming a peninsula, with the sea on the south side and Milford Haven to the North.

The actual Mess was down at the East end of the village, in a large requisitioned country house set in extensive grounds, entitled 'The Hall' It was a delightful property with wide sweeping staircases, countless bedrooms, a few bathrooms, lounges and a bar named 'The Stagger Inn'.

Many years later, on a return visit, I was introduced to The Cellar, guess it must have been boarded up or out of bounds when we were there lest its huge stock of vintage wines 'disappeared'.

Perhaps the most satisfying benefit I enjoyed was the shared services of a 'bat man'. No more worrying about laundry, shoe cleaning, uniform button polishing, bed making, sweeping and dusting. He was everything a bat man should be, and more. These were very special times.

Jumping ahead a little to the 15th May 1944 I approached the C.O. and explained that I would very much like to hold a 21st Birthday Party but did not feel that I could as according to the RAF, I would be twenty two. He was sympathetic but stressed that it was far too late for anyone to be concerned about my transgression on enlistment and to proceed with a grand slam 21st, which I did.

At about this time, speculation about a 'Second Front' in Europe was rife and we even had a huge map of Europe on the notice board in the upper Dining Room. We each pinned a tiny flag onto the spot where we guessed an invasion would take place at a cost of five shillings each (25 pence).

The flags covered much of the south coast of France, in the Mediterranean, all of the areas around the Channel Ports but NOT ONE appeared on the Normandy beaches. Not, that is, until just prior to D-Day.

In the run-up to D-Day, Milford Haven was swamped. As we climbed the slope up from 'The Hall' to our Dining Room on the Airfield, we always stopped to admire the view of the Haven. One morning, it all changed, as far as the eye could see to the East and to the West, the Haven was literally full of naval vessels. It appeared that an entire fleet and more had assembled, virtually overnight. At this point, my memory fails.I am totally unsure of the date and of how long they were there for. It must have been about the 2nd June and I think it was only on one morning that we saw them. We realised then that the invasion was imminent.

About this time, one of our senior officers flew up to Coastal Command HQ and, following his return on the 5th June, a solitary flag appeared in the area of the Normandy beaches. On the 6th he collected his winnings, insisting that it was purely 'intuition' and nothing whatsoever to do with his visit to the very centre of operations immediately prior to the landings! But, this was well into the future and I need now to wind the clock back to the previous autumn.

After a hugely busy September, the next month was almost restful with only eighteen flights, mainly in Wellingtons with pilots Flt Lts Ainsworth, Blackmore, Howeth and Mervyn-Smith. There were five flights in Hudsons and one in a Beaufighter with the C.O. (I seemed to have graduated to being his personal Wireless Operator).

This particular flight was called 'Fighter Affiliation', ducking and diving in and out of cloud cover with a spot of aerobatics; all great fun! I am not sure of the real purpose of the flight but it was most enjoyable.Other airfields landed at during the month included Colerne, Farnborough, Filton, Haverfordwest, Holmesly South and Northolt. The trials that I was involved with were coded 'Greenbottle' and 'Snowflakes', Mark III ASV, training and tactics, the Mark IX Bombsight, Night Photography, mock Leighlight attacks on a submarine and the Mark III Low Level bomb sight. Some of our 'runs' were on St. Bride's Bay bouy, Angle itself, Grassholme and Lundy Island.

November comprised seventeen flights, all bar two in Wellingtons, with Flt Lts Ainsworth and Blackmore. The odd two were with Flt Lt Mervyn Smith in a Liberator. Whilst taking off on the 3rd at 1803 hours in Wellington XII MP638 (M), the pilot's escape hatch opened up, necessitating a very quick circuit and landing in the dark; the first of quite a few 'spooky' happenings in the following months.

Our experiments were quite extensive. On the morning of the 3rd, whilst testing the Mark III Low Level Bomb Sight, along with Leigh Light manipulation, we dropped a total of twenty seven bombs. The only coded trial that month was 'Jellyfish'.

Other airfields, visited for various reasons included Farnborough, Haverford West, Northolt and St. Mawgan. A second trip to Northolt on the 18th enabled me to enjoy just a short overland journey from London to Southampton for a fortnight's leave. There was no such luck on the return trip; all the way to the very end of South Wales by rail. Only those who travelled by rail during the Second World War could know just how dreadful such journeys could be, particularly when endured in non-corridor, third class carriages. Although I have to admit, that after being commissioned, the relative comfort of First Class rail travel was enjoyed!

Then to December, and yes, before 'owt else', we were in the air on the afternoon of Christmas Eve plus twice on the 27th, on the 28th, twice on the 29th and on the 30th and the 31st. Christmas just 'came and went' in a hurry. Quite a few different trials were involved, including coded Greenbottle, Pumpkin, Snowflakes and my own 'Wirebasket'. Also MKII ASV, High Level photography from 13,000 feet in a Wellington, down sun attacks on a submarine, A.P.I test, photos of Depth Charge attacks and both 1.7" and 4" flares from a Halifax. In a later month such a trial ended in disaster when. on a night time flare trial, one became wedged in the chute and set fire to the aircraft, in full view of all the spectators on the cliff, visiting families, the crew's relatives; it was possibly the most horrible night of my life. The entire crew perished in front of their loved ones.

Airfields I landed at included Beaulieu, Carew Cheriton, Chivenor, Ford, Gosport, Haverfordwest, Holmsley South and Talbenny.

There were three incidents in the month. On the 14th the port generator was u/s, airborne for just fifteen minutes. On the 23rd, the port inner engine of a Halifax cut on take off, we hastily circuited and landed. Finally, on the 27th, in the same Halifax, the Air Speed Indicator failed on take off. The usual hasty return to 'Terra Firma' followed.

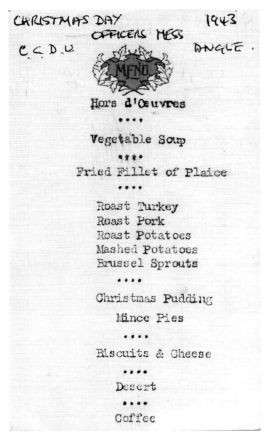

CCDU Officers Mess Christmas Day 1943 menu with all mess officers signatures on rear

From top clockwise; Catalina IVb, Ventura V, Wellington XIV and Halifax II

The final flight, on New Year's Eve, was the air testing of our 'unlucky' Halifax HR672 (K) when, for good measure, the SE just had to become unserviceable and force us to return to base.

Perhaps 1944 would see an improvement, so I hopefully thought! At least it started well with my promotion to flying officer on the 4th January and an increase of 3/9d in my daily pay to 18/3d.

After some trial work in the early part of the month, including a Navigation Exercise to Plymouth and the Isles of Scilly, (in the mighty Sunderland III, DP190 (T) 270 Squadron, pilot Fg Off Thompson) with me operating the SE, I was selected by the C.O. to act as Wireless and SE Operator on Liberator V FL958 (E) with Flt Lt Mervyn Smith as Captain and Wg Cdr Anstead as second pilot.

We were to take some very, very senior officers from Coastal Command HQ out to Gibraltar, North Africa, Naples, back to Gibraltar and then out into the Atlantic to the Azores. The object was for them to see at first hand how the Mediterranean Gee Chain operated; this was a fairly new Radar navigational aid.

We set off at noon on the 14th and initially flew down to RAF St Eval in Cornwall to top up our fuel tanks in readiness for what was, in those days, in 1944, a very long flight to Gibraltar. At 1500 hrs in the morning of the 15th, the adventure began and it took a full nine and a half hours to make the trip. Today you can reach Chicago and beyond in that time, even San Francisco under the best conditions. Gibraltar from Cornwall nowadays takes what? Three and a half hours, if that.

My first instinct, after arriving and settling in at the Officers Mess, was to go for a swim in the Med. Locals thought me crazy - to them it was mid-winter, to us it seemed spring-like. We enjoyed over two full days on 'The Rock', departing for Algiers on the morning of the 19th and arriving at the Maison Blanche airfield over three hours later.

The so-called 'runway' comprised metal sheets laid on top of the sand and the noise on landing was deafening, not to mention very disturbing as it was so unexpected. It sounded as though we were crash-landing! We only stayed one night, but what a night that proved to be! There were four junior officers in the crew and, as soon as we could politely depart from the main party, we headed into Algiers and found our way to the Casbah, only to find prominent notices proclaiming that it was well and truly 'Out of Bounds' to all ranks. Undeterred, we pressed on, climbing higher and higher into and through, a labyrinth of narrow, cobbled streets and alleyways, always virtually surrounded by local children with men, in full Arab attire, hovering a few yards away.

There was a commotion as a two wheel cart, drawn by a donkey, knocked over one of the children and a wheel went over the poor child's leg. There was pandemonium, the child's screams, the driver screaming that it was not his fault and then suddenly, a shout and an arm with an accusing finger was pointed at us from the crowd. It only takes a moment, in a 'mob' situation, for a serious state of affairs to arise and then to get out of hand. The four of us instinctively knew that we were about to be 'mobbed'.

One of us must have said 'Draw revolvers' and seconds later we were in full retreat, two facing forwards and two facing the rear, trying to return down the many steps without falling over but needing to maintain a fast speed. By occasionally shouting and making threatening gestures with our six shooters, we held them at bay and, as we moved down into a normal street, a couple of American Military Police appeared and, after saluting, told us how unwise we had been. We advised them that we had just arrived from England and they were duly sympathetic, even directing us to a large building with a massive wrought iron gate, where they inferred that we could get a drink and find solace.

It turned out to be a famous brothel, luxurious with thick carpets, gorgeous drapes, elegant furniture and a wee bar. One of us must have enquired about costs and, when we pooled our entire, but modest, wealth there was just sufficient for one of us to mount the huge, wide staircase leading to the upper floor.

It was soon agreed that the oldest member of the party, a Newfoundlander, should be our representative on the assumption that he might be more experienced than the rest of us. I think we three non-participants were too unsure of ourselves to become involved. So off he went with one of the very glamorous 'ladies' and it seemed no time at all before he came back down, with her following, protesting most loudly that he was quite useless and one of us should have gone instead. He never lived it down!

We were about to depart when there was a commotion at the entrance and our senior officers bundled in, accompanied by our C.O. They really had enjoyed their dinner at the airfield and had obviously imbibed too freely afterwards. The 'Madame' would have none of it - they were far too boisterous for her establishment and two super large Algerians quickly shepherded our 'Top Brass' out through the wrought iron gate. We waited a few moments, then quickly slipped away ourselves. I have no recollection of how we managed to get back to Maison Blanche, but we did.

On our return, we heard that there were problems at Naples and that it would be unwise of us to fly there, so the next day, the 19th, we flew back to Gibraltar in just under three hours. We stayed there a further two days and finally left at 0200 hours on the 22nd for an eight hour flight to the Azores, to RAF Lagens on Terceira. It was so difficult, nearly sixty five years later, to comprehend the huge length of time that it took in the 1940s to complete journeys that we now look up as short haul flights.

We enjoyed two full days at Lagens and I met up with many 206 personnel, the squadron having been posted there just after I had finished my tour of duty. Although they had only been in the Azores a very short while, there were still a lot of 'unhappy bunnies', with lots of the ground crew sleeping under hedgerows. Even the officers were not allowed the comfort of the Portuguese Officers Mess. I was asked if I could take back the odd three ply box to the UK and post it to the sender's girl friend or parents. It would be just large enough to house a pineapple which had been unheard of in the UK since 1939. Of course I agreed.

Sometime before take off, in the very early hours of the 22nd, the C.O. came to me and demanded to know why our Liberator had dozens (or was it hundreds) of wee three ply boxes, all addressed to UK houses, jammed into every 'nook and cranny' in the aircraft! Actually 'tis a wonder that there was space for them as at Gibraltar, someone had arranged for the purchase of enough Wine and Spirits to keep the various Messes at Angle stocked far into the future.

We were airborne at 0200 hrs and landed at Angle eight and three quarter hours later on the 25th. I heard, afterwards, that we had been advised to land at another airfield where there was a Customs post. I think we probably replied that our fuel situation would not

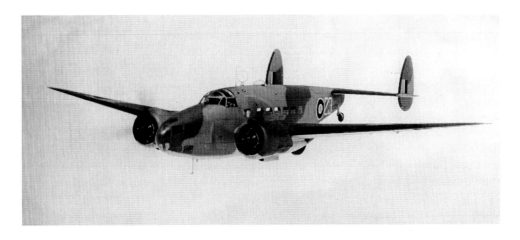

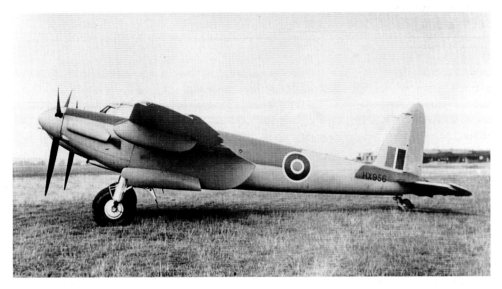

From top clockwise; Hudson V, Warwick GR.V, Mosquito FB.VI and Liberator GR.VIII

allow this. The MT section was waiting for us as we landed and most of our stocks of liquor and cigarettes were dispersed with great speed. We obviously left some on board so that when the Customs Officer, probably from Pembroke Dock, arrived, he was able to do his duty.

I heard, later, that the Mess profits proved to be so healthy in the following months that we paid the rest of the duty in full, no questions asked! The cost of posting all the pineapples came out of the Mess funds.

Reality soon took over and, on the 31st we set off in a Ventura V FN989(C) for Long Kesh, Northern Ireland, with Flt Lt Handasyde as pilot. We were to carry out a series of Radar trials down the Mull of Kintyre, in Kilbrannon Sound and also in Loch Fyne. It was a strenuous but enjoyable detachment, returning to Angle on the 8th February consisting of a total of six flights with the trial ones averaging about three and a half hours each. My last flight in February was on the 17th so I must have gone on leave between then and my next flight on the 2nd March, although I have no record of this, nor any recollection of it.

CCDU remained at Angle until the middle of January 1945 and during the remaining ten and a half months, I flew on one hundred and forty three flights, totalling in excess of two hundred and sixty flying hours. I also enjoyed time on board the submarine HMS *United* as detailed in Chapter 10.

Probably the best trials were those of R.P's; there truly is an exhilaration beyond words when flying in a smallish aircraft, such as a Beaufighter, with only the pilot and you on board and climbing steadily to operating height. To then locate the target, see the nose of the aircraft dip and away you go, counting the seconds before firing, usually in two batches, and then hearing the huge 'whoosh' as the rockets are released.

There were so many other trials which were less exciting but really worthwhile, and they filled every day. There were also quite a few incidents, some quite 'hairy' to say the least but, as I mentioned earlier, I was being 'watched over' and survived them all.

We flew out of Angle on the 14th January 1945, after over sixteen months, the longest I had ever spent at any airfield. In the event, apart from the C.O. and Adjutant, I was the longest serving member of the Unit's Aircrew.

On a return visit to the village of Angle on the 7th and 8th September 2003, I met up with an archivist and an historian. They were delighted to meet someone who had been there with CCDU and I was able to fill in a lot of 'blanks'. It was only on the rarest of occasions that any of the CCDU personnel visited the village and they never discussed any of the work we were doing as it was all classified and TOP SECRET. It was very satisfying to hear, after all those years, that the locals had no idea at all of what we were doing up there on our cliff top airfield. Secrets can be kept!

The organisation required to move such a large Unit from the far west of Wales to an airfield on the South Coast was massive. It involved, first of all, an Advance Party of ten, comprising a total of five officers and five NCOs, under the command of Sqn Ldr Westlake whose tasks were to arrange all the necessary quarters at Thorney Island, receive the main parties on their arrival, be responsible for the safe custody of equipment and generally co-ordinate and ensure the smooth running of movements at Thorney. This group left earlier than anyone else, by rail.

The main air party comprised thirty-three aircrew and thirteen ground crew and flew out on the 14th January in eight aircraft. There were three Wellingtons, one with me on

The author in Spring 1944

board, three Beaufighters and two Liberators. Our other aircraft had either been flown to Thorney earlier on, or disposed of. There were also seven Lancasters, comprising the Engine Control Instructional Flight, recently attached to us, they carried forty two aircrew and eleven ground crew.

The main party consisted of six officers and one hundred and forty two other ranks who travelled by train from Pembroke Dock to Emsworth Station. There was also a road party, comprising one officer and thirteen drivers and passengers, travelling in seven Lorries loaded with most of our personal equipment. The rear party, one officer and thirteen other ranks, followed when the site was finally handed over. Nearly three hundred personnel were involved and, looking back, I realise I had no idea that there were so many of us.

This was indeed a significant advance on my early days when we had about a couple of dozen aircrew, with a maximum of six WOP/AGs. The details of the move show that these numbers had doubled in the sixteen months in order to cope with the growing volume of trials we had to undertake.

In fact, this was partly the reason for the transfer to Thorney Island. We needed a much bigger aerodrome with improved facilities and we needed to be closer to places like Farnborough and Boscombe Down. We also needed to be nearer to Portsmouth and the English Channel as we were to be joined by the Fleet Air Arm and be re-named Air Sea

The much needed social seen with the author front (third from the left) and the commanding officer, Wg Cdr Anstead over Ted's left shoulder

Warfare Development Unit (ASWDU) Before we close the chapter on Angle it might be worth looking at the logistics of the move;

Advance Party. Took all of their personal kit.

Main Air Party. Personal kit restricted to one kit bag or suitcase. Tool kits to be taken. Surplus kit deposited as per main party.

Main Ground Party. Overnight gear only. Other personal kit to be deposited at one of five Sites, clearly labelled.

Road Party. Personal Kit. Some of officers' heavy luggage.

Rear Party. Personal kit and tools.

Equipment. Some equipment and stores were ferried by air prior to the move. Four 6 ton vehicles transferred the rest from Angle to Pembroke in stages.

    A from Hangar, Workshop, Armoury, Instrument and Electrical

    B from Hangar, Flight, ECIF and Stores. Photographic and Safety Equipment.

    C Radar. CCDU HQ. All Secret Equipment, Stores and Miscellaneous equipment.

    Luggage. To be collected from the 5 designated sites and taken by lorries to the railway station and loaded onto the train carrying the main party.

    Tankers, etc; 3 x 900 gallon tankers and 2x tractors. The tankers to be towed to Pembroke Station by the tractors with a crew available for loading onto the train.

    Safes; Four to be taken with HQ equipment.

    Rations; Road Party. Rations for 2½ days, Sandwiches for one day. Main Party. A meal before departure and one on arrival. One day's ration of sandwiches to be taken. Tea to be served en-route.

It was a momentous occasion, almost unique in that, when a squadron moved, the baggage mainly comprised of personal kit and tools with most of it flying out with the aircraft and aircrew. In this move we were taking everything, so much of which would normally belong to the Station and not the Unit. As Angle was a Satellite, this did not apply.

Chapter 10
Aboard HMS *United* P44

W hilst on rest on the Coastal Command Development Unit at Angle, South Wales, I was privileged to be selected to join one of His Majesty's submarines, the *United* on a liaison exercise.

The P44, skippered by Lt. Wood RN, was berthed at Pembroke Dock and I was transported there by road very early on the morning of the 18th June 1944, just twelve days after D-Day.

Quite a number of the trials we were involved in on the Unit concerned the locating of and locking on to submarines and this was to be an opportunity for the RAF to have on board an experienced trialist and Coordinator during a series of exercises. In other words to ensure that all the events taking place when submerged proceeded exactly as previously planned. Not only straightforward happenings such as engine idling, slow, medium and fast revolutions, loud talking, music and on board announcements, etc., but also various artificial noises such as dropped spanners, banging on metal objects, pounding the inner surfaces and many, many more.

We were submerged for eighteen hours, keeping a very close check on the exact timing of each incident during the entire trip. Above us, various aircraft, fitted with a variety of detectors, some old, some new, flew throughout the day tracking our every move, our changes of direction, our changes in depth and most of all trying to locate us when everything was switched off and we were motionless. The recording of the exact times was critical to the success of the operation.

As often happens, I was so busy with my many duties that I had no time to be concerned with when the last hatch was battened down and we submerged, in fact, it happened without my being aware of it. The confined space of the submarine was again not a cause for concern as I was quite used to flying in the confined space of aeroplanes such as the Avenger, the Beaufighter, the Mosquito and not least the Fairy Battle.

HMS United 'Spent 18 hours submerged' June 1944

It proved to be an exhausting trip and, after mooring at a bouy in Pembroke Dock on our return, I had to literally walk the tight rope. The Navy let me struggle out of the conning tower onto the deck where I expected to see a liberty boat waiting to take me ashore. But the Navy had thought otherwise as the liberty boat was secured to the forward buoy, meaning that I had to negotiate the very narrow and slippery gangway all the way from the conning tower, with my kit suspended from my shoulders. Mercifully, I <u>did not</u> slip and fall in, so once I was safely aboard the small liberty boat there was a great cheer from the conning tower. The RAF's reputation had been saved.

At a 206 Association Reunion in 2008 we were taken on a full tour of the submarine on permanent display at Gosport and I felt quite at home, almost nostalgic. But, as with HMS *Keppel* in 1942, I was quite happy to have been a flier and not a submariner.

Chapter 11

Non-Ops Flying ASWDU Thorney Island

Thorney Island, just outside Emsworth in Hampshire, was a top quality, modern RAF aerodrome. It had recently been vacated by the 2nd Tactical Air Force on its move to more forward airfields on the continent, as the Allied land advances progressed.

The quarters for all ranks were up to a high standard whilst the Officers Mess was a dream, after the split arrangements at Angle and the Nissen huts on Benbecula. I shared a room with Flt Lt Leo Ross, an American serving in the RAF. He mainly piloted Liberators but was adept at anything. I flew with him in an Anson, a Proctor, a Reliant and a Walrus plus of course the Liberators; he was a man of many talents with whom I became a close friend.

More of this later, first of all, what was planned for the future of our newly named Air Sea Warfare Development Unit in the months to come? Perhaps an extract or two from 'A Simple Guide for the Staff' issued in 1946, after the war had ended and just before I was demobilised, might clarify our role. (Bear in mind that we moved to Thorney in January 1945.)

Objects of the unit

1. The name ASWDU to a large extent speaks for itself but we will enlarge on it briefly and simply.
2. As aircraft weapons and instruments have become so numerous and complicated it is necessary for each of the main operational or potentially operational commands to have units which can decide or recommend not only which weapons or equipments are best

for a particular form of warfare, but also how to employ them to the best advantage. This unit, originally known as Coastal Command Development Unit, serves Coastal Command and consequently any similar commands overseas.

3. Most of our work will come under one of the following five categories:-

   (a) Trying out weapons to assess their value in attacks on sea targets.

   (b) Finding the best technique for using weapons against sea targets, i.e. developing the tactical application of the weapons.

   (c) Helping the designers of 'gadgetry' to advise ways of improving them to best suit the users.

   (d) Working out the best drills for navigation, radar, signals and photography in maritime aircraft.

   (e) Improving methods of air-sea rescue.

4. Consider the following figures of the war against U-boats during the European phase of the Second World War. Out of a total number of 740 U-boats known to have been destroyed as a result of direct attacks by aircraft and ships, 399 went to ships alone, out of which number 72 were accounted for by our own submarines. This leaves 289 to the credit of air attack and 52 were shared by ships and aircraft. We cannot claim to have sunk any U-boats ourselves, but the Unit made a good contribution to the factors leading up to the enormous success of air power against the submarine.

Not long after our arrival, our C.O. Wg Cdr Anstead (also C.O. at Angle), had an increased complement including two squadron leaders, twenty one flight lieutenants, fourteen flying officers and four pilot officers. We also had five technical officers, (Engineering, Armament, Signaling and Admin.) There were only six non-commissioned aircrew then.

Of the forty eight aircrew, eighteen were pilots, nine navigators, four flight engineers and seventeen wireless op/air gunners. This was a significant advance from my early days at Angle when the total strength was half that number, with a maximum of half a dozen WOP/AGs.

It was a couple of weeks before I was involved in trial work, maybe we were 'settling in' or maybe I enjoyed a spot of leave before work started in earnest on the 29th January. We began with runs on Portland Bill, though these were aborted due to bad weather, so we were only airborne for an hour and a half.

February involved sixteen separate flights, the first one in Wellington HF206 XIV(D), lasting only twenty five minutes as the Starboard engine failed. My Angle jinx had followed me to Thorney!

We were detached to East Fortune in Scotland on two occasions in the month, for seven days and then for nine days. Three of the transit flights each took two and a quarter hours but the first one was nearly half an hour longer. On each of the four I acted as Map Reader, so maybe on the first one I led the pilot astray! Whilst at East Fortune we were wholly involved in Radar Trails, using Mark VI and Lucero-type 942 in homing runs onto HMS *Pollux* (Radar training ship). The reason for our return after the initial trip was down to RADAR u/s and LUCERO u/s. Once they were both repaired we returned north and were trialing for several hours each day with myself being responsible for all the radar work, again with HMS *Pollux* as our target.

From to clockwise; Swordfish, Barracuda, Walrus and Avenger

On our return to Thorney toward the end of the month, we were mostly involved with Snorkel searches; again using Mark VI radar, the snorkel being the small breathing pipe used by submarines which was very, very difficult to locate. We spent quite a while in the vicinity of Cherbourg whilst on these trials.

March was busy until the middle of the month when I think I might possibly have gone on leave as there are no entries after the 15th. I had flown in the 'work-horse' Wellington in the main, but also in the Anson, the Liberator and the Warwick, mainly on trials with the Mark VI Radar and the Mark XV Bomb sight and had completed fifteen hundred flying hours on the 7th of the month.

April was again busy with twenty four flights, including visits to Gosport and Farnborough in the Avro Anson plus an interesting variety of other aircraft from the powerful Liberator, Warwick, Wellington, Avenger, Barracuda and Proctor to the Fleet Air Arm's Swordfish. I enjoyed four flights in the 'String bag' and if you ever want to really enjoy flying, this is the 'plane. An open cockpit, whistling wind, slipstream noise and when you get down to sea level and race along the South Coast, literally 'beating up' the beaches and waving to the odd walker, that's flying! For a twenty one year old, that's bliss!

We had done some serious trial work with one of my projects code named 'Wirebasket' but on this occasion we had a fault and were returning from recalling the launch. This vessel was used to retrieve our 'gadgetry' after we had dropped them into the English Channel and then tried to locate each one with our radar, Rebecca IIb.

On the 17th, we were airborne for just ten minutes in a Wellington, piloted by Fg Off Cowan, as the petrol flaps flew open and the starboard engine failed. I was becoming quite used to single engine landings! I flew on nearly every day that month. Well, I said it was busy!

Of course, the best month of the war was May itself with twenty two flights including one with Leo Ross in a Reliant; it was the first time he had flown one! There were also three flights with Leo in a Walrus, again a first for him! We did some trial photography then called in at Calshot to find out if he could land it near the slipway and actually 'drive' up it. He was an amazing man. We did a lot of work with 'Wirebasket' and my second major project, 'Walter', another Air Sea Rescue aid.

On the 3rd May, our Wellington (Pilot Flt Lt Urlwyn-Smith DFC) was struck by lightning and we hastily returned to base and safety. At 0241 hours on the 7th, the German Armed Forces surrendered unconditionally and the following day was declared to be VE Day, Victory in Europe Day and, at 1500 hours, the European War officially ended.

There was little time to celebrate as at 1100 hours on the 9th, I was again airborne on a 'Walter' trial, and in any case the war in the Far East was still blazing away. I flew in seven different types of aircraft in the month, mainly concerned with my two projects.

June was interesting, there were five different types of aircraft and an amazing six and a half hour flight on so called 'Range Flying', from Thorney Island along the coast to Dover, across the Channel to Calais then along the French and Dutch coasts to Denmark, inland to the almost totally destroyed cities of Hamburg and Bremen which were absolutely breathtaking sights, then homeward via Rotterdam. To see so much damage wherever we flew on the Continent, just a month or so after the end of the European War, was a most unforgettable experience.

Then came another memorable few days when we had heard that there was an eighteen foot, half deck, clinker built sailing boat for sale by an RAF type in the Isles of Scilly and, on the afternoon of the 23rd June, Leo and I decided to take the Walrus down there to inspect it. Our Flight Commander, Sqn Ldr Pete Holmes DFC Bar joined us, together with a WAAF officer and a recently released POW. A likely bunch!!

Pete Holmes took off at 1515 hours and flew it down to Predannock in Cornwall for refuelling, which was a two and a half hour journey, it was probably the first time he had ever piloted a Walrus. At 1845 hrs we took off again with Leo at the controls. After half an hour, we sighted the islands and located the minute airfield at St Mary's. We circled it a couple of times and voted unanimously that it looked far too small for a novice Walrus pilot to safely land our machine. It was agreed that we would attempt a landing in the bay but there were too many small boats dotted here and there for comfort.

So it had to be the sea, outside the harbour. This was a huge risk, not easy with a swell, even for an experienced Walrus pilot, for a Gung-Ho! American, almost new to the type, it could have been disastrous. But fortune favours the brave and so we all gave him the 'thumbs up' and in we went. Literally! There were waves everywhere and an awful lot of noise. As we slowed down after landing, we tilted to port with the wing tip nearly in the sea. Our ex POW climbed out onto the starboard wing to balance it a little and we crept laboriously toward the St Mary's harbour, finally being met by an RAF launch and guided to a buoy. Leo had unfortunately smashed the port float on touch down so we were in serious difficulties and a long, long way from home.

The next day, I sat in a small row-boat under the port wing, pulling desperately on the oars to keep her so positioned that Leo and Pete could attempt to stabilise the float with lashings. I think I became more sun-tanned in one day than ever before or since.

The RMV 'Scillonian' leaves the Isles of Scilly

In the event we purchased the boat on behalf of the Officers Mess and, some time later, it appeared at Emsworth Station on a flat bottom rail car. In the meantime, we needed to get back to Thorney in a hurry so left the Walrus behind, sailed across to Penzance on the 'Scillonian', secured transport to RAF Portreath where, miraculously, a Thorney Island Proctor had appeared for Leo to fly us all back to base that evening.

Sqn Ldr Holmes appeared before the station commander the next morning with Leo, the WAAF officer, the ex POW and me in the outer office. He explained to us afterwards that we could have been 'Court Martialed' and indeed still would be if word of our escapade ever leaked out. We were literally sworn to secrecy but as it would be difficult to locate any survivors of that period sixty years on I guess my detailing it now is permissible.

I have no record of ever flying in the Walrus again, nor have I any knowledge of her subsequent activities. She would doubtless have been repaired and duly flown out to a new home, well away from Leo's grasp. The boat was finally transported to the end of a jetty near the Officers Mess and became the very first sailing boat owned by the Officers Mess, newly formed Sailing Club. We had huge fun in her, often sailing round to the many other jetties which abounded, often with a small pub nearby. Bosham was our favourite but Bosham Hoe, West Itchenor, Birdham and Dell Quay also featured. These were indeed halcyon days.

In July, my promotion to Flight Lieutenant came through on the 4th which meant I was now earning 21/9d a day, just over £7.00 a week. Indeed a princely sum! On the 27th, I made my first flight with a Sqn Ldr Dart DFC in a Barracuda when we flew over to Tangmere and later in the day trialed 'Walter'. On the 31st, I flew with him again in a Warwick, testing the Barb Sight whilst taking evasive action. We seemed to strike up a partnership as I was again up with him on a similar exercise on the 1st August and on the 31st August, we took a crowd of Naval Cadets in a Liberator around the area, in particular showing them the *Queen Elizabeth* in Southampton Docks.

Lancaster RE164 served with the ASWDU as a ASR.3 but is seen here many years later after conversion to a GR.3

I mention all this detail as, shortly afterwards, he crashed our only Mosquito near Tunbridge Wells and was killed outright.He managed to keep her under control long enough to avoid crashing in the middle of the village of Rusthall but finally came down within a few yards of the Senior girl's school. Two girls were slightly hurt, others had their hair singed. No further comment is needed.

But to return to the famous month of August 1945, when, on the 15th, at 0001 hours, the World War terminated with the Japanese accepting our surrender offer; there were massive celebrations.

Between VE and VJ days a whole new life began for me. Neither of us remembers the exact date but it was after Ona's 17th birthday, so possibly at the end of March or more probably on my next leave at the end of June/early July. Doris Peters, as she then was, had it noted in her diary but she took the decision to burn all of them only weeks before we phoned and asked her for the detail early in 2008, about the time of our Diamond Wedding celebration.

However, before we delve further into this new aspect of my life, the Thorney Island part has to be concluded. ASWDU continued apace and 'Walter' occupied most of September when I enjoyed only my second flight in a Catalina, piloted by Flt Lt Stockwell DFC. There were only six flights, even less in October, inter airfield flights to Farnborough on the 8th and 9th. November was concentrated on 'K' band ASV in a Warwick, and for the very first time, a Lancaster. Flt Lt Hamilton DFC piloted us on a photographic trip around Southampton Docks.

December was not much better, with only five flights incorporating IFF Corner Reflectors and the Mark VI A, Truant.

1946 dawned, when I flew mainly in Wellingtons and Liberators although I did enjoy a second flight in a Lancaster. Trials included Corner Reflectors, Mark VI b bombing, identification of Surface Craft and checking suitability of buoys for snorkel trials. On the 24th, we located a floating mine and, on the 30th, we made a hasty return to Thorney Island when our Radar equipment burst into flames.

February was relatively uneventful except that on the 15th we had to return to base as the bombs we had on board for trial would not release from our Wellington bomb bay. We were mainly trialing the Mark VI b, including some night flying. There were only nine flights in the month.

For some reason, March showed an improvement with fifteen flights, mainly concerned with Mark VIb bombing and Centimetre IFF. There were two events of note. On the 20th we had to return to base whilst on an Air Test as the petrol tanks produced problems, making the aircraft unserviceable; whilst on the 30th March I had my very last, my absolutely final flight with the RAF, a one and a half hour Radar Trial in a Wellington XIII NC152 (E), Pilot Flt Lt Pulleyn, from 1035 'til noon.

So, after 1,657 hours and 40 minutes flying time on seven hundred and seventeen flights, with one hundred and twenty five different pilots and in twenty five different aircraft, landing at seventy two different airfields, it all began to unwind. But it was not until the 14th May 1946 that I was finally 'withdrawn from Aircrew Duties', still just twenty two years of age, by a day!

Apart from my brief stay at Benson in June 1941, my log-books confirm that, from my very first flight at Cranwell on the 1st May 1941 until this last one on the 30th March 1946, I had flown during every single calendar month, so no wonder there was a story waiting to be told.

It was in a Vickers Wellington XIII that Ted made his 717th Flight and last in an RAF aircraft

My last effective day of service is recorded as being the 20th June 1946, virtually six years from the day I enlisted. Let us now rewind to the 'Month of our Meeting' (Ona and I) about which we will never be certain. So let us think generally of the early Spring of 1945, sometime after March 9th, Ona's 17th Birthday.

I was on leave in Southampton; not a very exciting situation, as everything, what little there was, closed down at 10 pm. There were, maybe, three or four cinemas, a couple of dance halls and a few pubs open.So I went to the Guildhall, where you could dance from 6 to 10 pm, six nights a week. This was my first visit I would add. Not so with Ona, she went there five times a week at least and had done so for quite a while, probably since she was sixteen. She learned more about dancing in that year or so than you would normally learn in a lifetime. This even included 'Jitter bugging' with so many American Army and Air Force lads stationed in or near Southampton.

But this was a special night. She was with a party of seven or eight other girl friends, mainly from Tyrell and Green's and resolutely announced to them that she was 'fed up' with these Americans. She was 'fed up' with their many airy promises, usually concerning their assured return to the UK after the war, to claim their 'bride to be'. She was going to 'find' a nice Englishman and, on sighting an RAF officer at the top of the stairs, leading down to a small bar, she said, "He'll do."

No one was more surprised than Ona when 'he' walked toward the group and asked her, in particular, if she would care to dance.

At the end of the evening, after a few more dances, it was agreed that I could walk her home the few hundred yards to the Park Inn in Pound Tree Road which was her parents very own public house! I could write another book on subsequent events and the ensuing sixty odd years, perhaps I will now that this one is almost complete. But I can only write now about events between our meeting and my departure from the RAF on demobilisation.

Obviously I saw her again and again when on leave and on hearing of her love of horse riding, even started buying the gear myself in readiness for some lessons! But all too soon it was VJ Day and our station commander decreed that we were to hold a celebratory Ball, a County Ball, but to be better by far than any pre-war event of its kind.

Aircraft were despatched, obviously on some 'training' pretext or other, to a variety of destinations which specialised in exotic food and drink. We needed barrels of Irish Guinness, oysters, fish, fruits, wine and liqueurs, often from far away sources and largely unobtainable in the UK.

The Mess was transformed into a wonderfully decorated 'hotel' with the huge entrance hall housing a massive silver Punch Bowl on an antique table, right in the middle. The billiard room tables were covered with protective boards and white linen tablecloths, and then filled with a host of delicacies. The bar was enlarged and the extensive lounge area became a ballroom.

Up in the Minstrels Gallery was an Oyster Bar, complete with the obligatory barrels of black Irish Guinness. The station band provided the music. Then I saw Ona coming up the steps at the main entrance. She had travelled by train to Chichester and to the hotel where she was spending a couple of nights, had changed and then came back to Thorney by taxi.

I was almost overwhelmed; she looked absolutely gorgeous in one of her Mother's many evening gowns. Bedecked with her Mother's jewellery and a small fur cape around her shoulders, she wore the highest of high heels. If I was not already in love with her I certainly 'fell' for her at that moment.

Before we had a chance to say much to each other, a couple of WAAF officers took over. They whisked her away to the powder room and took it in turns, with other WAAF officers, to chaperone her. I doubt if we had more than one dance together, she really was 'The Belle of the Ball'! At the end of the evening she was chaperoned back to her hotel in Chichester whilst I stayed in the Mess! All this at just seventeen and a half.

As previously detailed, there were still several months of 'trialing' ahead of me, but I am sure I must have fitted in quite a few visits to Southampton to see Ona again, before my final departure from Thorney and the RAF on the day before my twenty third birthday.

It had proved to be an eventful six years, on the whole worthwhile, and full of quite enjoyable experiences. It was often 'scary' but I had survived, just long enough to meet the lady with whom I have been fortunate enough to spend the ensuing sixty plus idyllic years.

Chapter 12
Demobilisation

At some time prior to demobilization, a small crowd of us took a double vow, possibly back in the Squadron days. We Vowed;

a) Never to fly again if we survived the war.
b) Never to be involved in a career which required us to be awakened in the small hours and to be 'on duty' before dawn.

I kept vow a) until 1980 but failed b) in the 1950s at Partridge Green, where I seemed to work all hours of the day and once worked through the night.

Reverting to the 'demob' itself, it was actually quite painless and so much time had passed since the end of the war that it became just a natural consequence. With such huge numbers of personnel leaving in stages, depending almost entirely on one's role at the time, farewell parties just did not happen. People 'drifted away' week after week, month after month. As I was still doing useful work, it was over a year from the end of the war in Europe to my final effective day of service.

The many stories you will have heard about demob suits were all true. It is now inconceivable that anyone could have agreed that retiring servicemen, who had unselfishly and often heroically served their country, should be issued with ill fitting suits made from the poorest quality material. They really were almost unwearable.I was able to retain my uniform, my flying gear and my massive camp kit, the only item 'they' really wanted back was my revolver, my inducement to enlist in 1940.

In fairness to the RAF, I must mention the efforts made to re-introduce me to civilian life, including a course at Southampton University. Primarily Economics, with one lecturer forecasting the end of Butchers' shops with rabbits and chicken hung up outside, of a host of other retail outlets being replaced by American type general stores, to become known as 'Super' Markets. I could not, and would not, accept the idea that our shopping streets could be so transformed. How wrong can one be? There were also lectures on finance, local government and politics. I quite enjoyed it as it enabled me to see Ona every evening throughout the course!

One final mention, in 1947, after a few months back with H.J. Heinz, I was approached by my CCDU/ASWDU Flight Commander Sqn Ldr Pete Holmes who had opened up 'The London School of Air Navigation' to join with him and my old C.O. Wing Commander Anstead as their Accounts Manager, in their premises near Marble Arch. The offer was too good to refuse and so the three of us long standing CCDU/ASWDU types were in harness together once more. Guess I must have 'proved my worth' in the thirty three months that I flew with them.

The aftermath of the war will be covered in another book, sufficient to mention one further vow which I took on the 20th June 1946, to have nothing more to do with the RAF or anything associated with it. For the following fifty years, I kept that vow and had you known the state I was in when I left the RAF you would understand my reasoning.

Had it not been for Ona, then a really beautiful and very mature eighteen year old, and her Mother, nick named 'Tot' or 'Tottie', I might never have recovered from the bouts of stuttering and stammering which used to overcome me. This was possibly a nervous reaction to all those near misses, a reaction of necessity kept at bay whilst still flying. So exactly fifty years after being demobbed, I joined the Royal Air Force Association and immediately discovered that there was not only a 206 Squadron Association, but also that there was to be a reunion at the end of August at RAF Kinloss, way, way up on the North East coast of Scotland. Having spent the previous sixteen years flying all over the globe, a flight up to Aberdeen and thence by hire car was a 'doddle'.

This was followed by annual reunions, in 1997 at Cambridge, from where we visited RAF Oakington and Duxford Museumand were enthralled to see Fortresses again for the first time since 1943. Then, later, in 1997 to Benbecula, where we met up with Tom Blue and Jim Romanes, my old C.O. Our friendship with Mike Hughes began here in the September. This was a busy 206 Squadron year, as we also attended a luncheon at the RAF Club in Piccadilly.

1998 saw us at Lincoln where Ona enjoyed her first glider flight at the age of 70, plus another London luncheon. Before arriving at the Post House Hotel in Lincoln, and some miles away, we had driven past a sign post to Swinderby, where I had been stationed in 1940. I reminded Ona of the David Niven episode and later on during the early evening 'Meet and Greet', I again recounted the story to my fellow ex 206 guests. Towards the end of it I asked

'And who do you think was in the back of the car?'

There was a brief silence, then from the back of the lounge bar came the words, 'David Niven', and up stepped Brian Spence, my fellow 'hitch hiker', whom I had not seen since Benbecula in 1943, some fifty four years previous and the only other person in the world who could have made this reply!!

1999 took in Bath and an invitation to the Russian Embassy in London! This was a celebration of their Victory Day. There was a second visit to Benbecula with a major 'Battle of Britain' parade and flypast by a 206 Squadron Nimrod. 2000 included Newquay, 2002 York,

2004 Lincoln and St Omer, France, 2005 Shrewsbury, 2006 found us at Little Morwood, Bucks, conveniently placed for a day at the Bletchley Park museum where spying became computerised and 'Enigma' a household name. Then, later in the year we were at King's Lynn for a Bircham Newton unveiling ceremony.

2007 included RAF Aldergrove in Northern Ireland and Lytham St Anne's, including the BAE Systems factory at Warton. Then, in 2008, we were at Southsea and the Gosport Submarine Museum. 2009 will include a return visit to York which we hope we will be able to support.

It would be remiss of me not to include a little more detail of the two visits to Benbecula in 1997 and 1999 and to comment most favourably on the Caledonian MacBrayne vessels that we sailed in, a far cry from their war time predecessors.

In 1997 we flew to Glasgow from Heathrow (£64 return by British Airways), collected a hire care and drove up to and through the Western Highlands, calling in at Plockton, the home of a TV series, on the way to Ullapool. There we took the car across to the Western Isles by MacBrayne's most excellent ferry, landing at Stornoway on the Isle of Lewis. We drove right up to the Butt of Lewis then down through both Lewis and Harris to Leverburgh.

Another pleasant MacBrayne ferry took us to North Uist before the drive to Benbecula. After the reunion it was down to Loch Boisdale and another excellent ferry journey via Barra to Oban. Then we travelled by car to Edinburgh, where we lived in 1950, and then back to Glasgow for the flight home.

1999 was similarly trouble free. We went again to Glasgow, but from Bournemouth this time, and then by hire car up through Western Scotland to Oban. An excellent MacBrayne ferry sailing took us to the Isle of Mull and successful visits to Iona and then to Fingal's Cave on the Isle of Staffa.

We went from Tobermory on Mull to the mainland at Kilchoan by yet another MacBrayne ferry. Then by road again we travelled to Mallaig and then by ferry to Ardvasan on Skye. After touring the island MacBrayne's took us from Uig to Lochmaddy in the Outer Hebrides, from where we drove to Benbecula. After the massive reunion we sailed from Loch Boisdale to Barra, an amazing island with aircraft landing and taking off from the beach. Finally, we journeyed from Barra to Oban, by road to Glasgow and back to Knoll View. I cannot praise the MacBrayne steamers enough, I only wish we could do it all again.

So we are both well and truly back in the folds of the RAF, despite my fifty year Sabbatical. The war may seem just a part of history to many of you, but to us it was a major event in our lives and will always be remembered. Well, after all, it brought us both together and has resulted in a family of three children and seven grand-children. Including spouses and partners, we are now seventeen; Ona's age when we first met.

Thank you for reading my survivor's tale.

Chapter 13
Postscript

This has been the story of just one Englishman's war. It saddens me that it cannot include the detail of the heroics performed by Ona's brother Colin Shefferd. He saw WWII at close quarters, mainly through the visor of his armoured car. Perhaps it will be possible to secure from the Bovington Tank Museum the records of the interviews he gave to the historians and have them published.

I also regret that I was never able to persuade Bernard, the husband of Ona's late cousin Heather, to commit to paper the 'before and after' of D Day. He was one of the few to land on the night of the 5th June, before the invasion on the 6th. His task was the marking out of his section of the beach and he was, in effect, a Controller. He even had a letter signed by General Montgomery himself, telling everyone concerned that he, Naval Commando Bernard, spoke with the authority of the General. He really enjoyed that! It is so very sad that all of this is not on record as part of the family's history.

Then we have Geoff, Bernard's close friend, who made twenty seven bombing raids, preceded by a single familiarisation flight in the mighty Lancaster. He undertook twenty seven hazardous journeys bombing Germany, always with the odds stacked against him, but he survived. He could recount in detail the performances of his four engines on each trip as a Flight Engineer, but he never recounted the hazards or committed them to paper.

Reg, the husband of another of Ona's close cousins, Myrtle, was in the Merchant Navy in the Battle of the Atlantic and in the Far East. He too could write his own book of his never ending hazardous voyages. Yes, another family un-sung hero.

Similarly, we never hear from Norman, my elder sister's husband, not only about his UK exploits but about his time in Iceland.

Ona's Uncle George, elder brother of her mother and of whom she was very fond, was torpedoed on the 29th September 1940 and drowned. Again, there is nothing much else on record. He was forty two and had previously been torpedoed when on the S.S. *Britannic*, but survived that sinking. I think he was with an Army Marine unit when he was finally 'lost at sea'.

Staying with WWII, my own father was an ARP (Air Raid Precautions) Warden and his relatively early demise at seventy four was partly brought on his strenuous efforts, rescuing people from bomb damaged buildings during the many Air Raids on Southampton.

If we go back to WWI my father was in the Royal Garrison Artillery and I have two pictures which sum it all up. One, taken in 1916 on their arrival in France and features huge numbers of men. The second, on their return in 1918, is only of Post Card size.I have never been able to bring myself to do a head count; the disparity is too heart breakingly obvious.

Then we have Ona's Uncle Charles, her father's brother, who is remembered on the Southampton War Memorial for his part in WW1. There are no further details, but there ought to be, and I will make it my responsibility to find out more about his giving up his life for his country.

And last but not least, Ona's father, who ran away to sea on the outbreak of WW1 and endured so many years at constant risk. Blessed with good fortune, like his Son-in-law, he too survived.

I am so very proud of our families and their many contributions to our Nation's survival.

Appendices

Key

AA	Anti Aircraft
ASR	Air Sea Rescue
COL	Crashed on landing
COTO	Crashed on take off
DBR	Damaged beyond repair
FTR	Failed to Return
Dam.	Damaged

Appendix 1
Silloth

No.1 OTU Hudson Losses during 1941

Date	A/c No.	Cause of loss	Location
11 Feb	T9296	Crashed	Dumfries
17 Feb	T9267	COTO	Silloth
3 May	T9361	COL	Silloth
4 May	N7304	Ditched	Solway Firth
19 Jul	T9341	COL	Silloth
28 Jul	T9268	Ditched	Off Skinburness

The following three losses during the author's two months at Silloth

2 Aug	P5155	COL	Silloth
1 Sep	T9301	Ditched	Off Grune Point
9 Sep	N7337	Crashed into hill	Ramsey, I.O.M.
26 Oct	P5116	COL	Silloth
14 Nov	AM534	Ditched	Solway Firth
17 Nov	AM750	Crashed	
14 Dec	N7223	Crashed	Silloth
21 Dec	AM624	Crashed into hill	Egremont
28 Dec	AM786	Crashed	Maryport

Total Hudson losses suffered by No.1 OTU

1940	From 8 Jul	6 aircraft
1941		15 aircraft
1942		36 aircraft
1943	to September	17 aircraft
	Total losses	**74 aircraft**

Approximately one aircraft lost every two weeks

Appendix II
Aldergrove

206 Squadron Hudson Losses

April 1940 to July 1942

Date	A/c No.	Operation	Cause of loss	Location
1940				
25 Apr	N7403		COL Blew up	Bircham Newton
3 May	N7319	River Elbe	Dam by Me109 COL	Bircham Newton
12 May	N7353	Bactrum	Shot down by Me109	
18 May	N7400	Hamburg	FTR	
18 May	N7329	Hamburg	FTR	
20 May	N7363	Hamburg	FTR	
22 May	N7402	German Coast	FTR	
20 Jun	P5120		COL	Bircham Newton
29 Jun	N7299		COL	Bircham Newton
4 Jul	N7368	ASR Texel	FTR	
4 Jul	P5162	ASR Texel	FTR	
3 Aug	T9282		FTR	
5 Aug	P5133		Crashed, Blew up	Norfolk
5 Aug	T9272		COL DBR	Aldergrove
6 Aug	P5153		COL Blew up	Bircham Newton

Date	A/c No.	Operation	Cause of loss	Location
7 Aug	N7395		COL Blew up	Bircham Newton
14 Aug	N7401		COTO Docking	
1 Sep	N7367		COTO Blew up	Bircham Newton
3 Sep	N7351		COTO	Docking
7 Sep	T9276		COL	Bircham Newton
10 Oct	T9357		COL	Docking
14 Oct	N7362		FTR	
16 Oct	T9303		FTR	
10 Nov	T9382		Hit by AA abandoned	
19 Nov	N7300		Crashed in fog	Docking
20 Dec	N7333		COTO	Bircham Newton
1941				
1 Jan	T9287		Crashed, low flying	Langham
4 Feb	T9331		FTR	
12 Feb	T9289		FTR	
12 Feb	T9346		Abandoned in fog	Caithness
12 Feb	T9350		Abandoned in fog	Caithness
20 Mar	AE611		COTO	Aldergrove
21 Apr	T9304		Crashed	Castle on Dinas
17 May	T9324		Crashed	North Sheppey
12 Jun	AE614	ASR Search	FTR	
13 Jun	AE612	ASR Search	FTR	
1 Jul	AE609	Patrol	FTR	
8 Jul	AE613	ASR Patrol	Ditched	
16 Aug	AM588		Crashed into hill	Co. Antrim
24 Sep	AM664		COL	Aldergrove
11 Dec	AM634	ASR PATROL	Ditched	
21 Dec	AM837		FTR	
1942				
31 Jan	AM690		DBR	Aldergrove
1 Feb	AM604		Crashed into trees	Aldergrove
1 Feb	AM613		COTO	Aldergrove
5 Feb	AM706		COL	Aldergrove

Date	A/c No.	Operation	Cause of loss	Location
14 Feb	AM622		COTO Blew up	Aldergrove
Author on board				
8 Apr	T9431		COTO	Aldergrove
26 Jun	AM606	Bremen	FTR	
26 Jun	AM762	Bremen	FTR	
28 Jul	AM805	ASR Patrol	FTR	Benbecula

51 aircraft in just over two years. One every fortnight.

11 in the nine months during the author's tour at Aldergrove.

Appendix III

Benbecula

RAF operated Boeing Flying Fortress Losses 1941-1946

Approximately 155 Fortresses were delivered by the Americans to British Front Line Squadrons and were in operation between the 1st May 1941 and March 1945. They substantially increased the ability to make flights of nearly twice the time possible in the Lockheed Hudson.

As will be seen from the following detailed list of losses, they mainly went to the following Squadrons; 59, 90, 206, 214 and 220 with a few to 251 and 519, but in the main to the first five. So it is understandable that both during and after the Second World War most people found it difficult to accept that we actually flew in Fortresses. They were convinced that they were American Aircraft, flown by Americans on daylight bombing raids over Nazi occupied Europe.

More than a third of all the Fortresses delivered to these RAF Squadrons were lost, at a rate of about one per month, for a wide variety of reasons, FTR being high on the list.

Providentially, losses of Fortresses were not as high as those of the Hudsons.

Date	A/c No.	Sqn	Cause of loss	Location
1941				
22 Jun	AN522	90	Broke up	Catterick Bridge
3 Jul	AN528	90	Caught fire on ground	Polebrook
28 Jul	AN534	90	Broke up	Stoke Albany
16 Aug	AN523	90	Dam. by fighters; COL	Roborough
6 Sep	AN533	90	Shot down by fighters	Norway
8 Sep	AN525	90	Shot down by fighters	Norway

8 Sep	AN535	90	Dam. By fighters; COL	Kinloss
8 Nov	AN529	90	Crashed during forced landing	Libya
1942				
9 Jan	AN536	90	Broke up in cloud	Foxton
10 Jan	AN521	90/220	Engine caught fire, abandoned	Shallufa
10 Aug	FK207	220	Dived into ground	Nutts Corner
11 Aug	FK204	220	Ran out of fuel, abandoned	Acklington
6 Oct	FL454	206	Stalled on takeoff	Benbecula
12 Dec	FL453	206	FTR	Benbecula
1943				
23 Mar	FK209	53/59	FTR	
26 Mar	FA698	59	Crashed into hill	Chivenor
11 Jun	FA704	59/206	Ditched in the North Atlantic	
14 Jun	FK212	220	FTR	
25 Oct	FK202	59/220	Ditched	
29 Nov	FK208	206	Ditched	Gibraltar
4 Dec	FK206	220	Ditched after takeoff	
19 Dec	FA697	220	COL	
1944				
6 Jan	FA705	206	FTR	Azores
19 Apr	FK198	59/206/ 220	Hit by HB786 whilst parked	Azores
25 May	SR384	214	FTR	
22 Jun	SR381	214	DBR	
22 Jun	SR382	214	FTR	
26 Jul	FA707	206/ 220	Ditched	Azores
26 Jul	FK189	59/ 220	Caught fire on takeoff	Azores
2 Aug	FA706	220	Taxied into another aircraft	Azores
26 Aug	HB763	214	FTR	
29 Aug	FL451	206/251	COL	Aldergrove
12 Sep	SR380	214/1699	COL	Oulton
13 Sep	HB767	214	DBR	
7 Nov	HB788	214	FTR	
16 Nov	HB787	214	Crashed on approach	Foulsham

28 Dec	FK191	206/220	Overshot landing	Gosport
1945				
17 Jan	KJ103	214	Hit trees on approach	Oulton
22 Jan	FL462	59/ 220	Hit trees during overshoot	Gosport
1 Feb	FL455	206/519	Crashed into ground from cloud	Wick
9 Feb	HB796	214	FTR	
24 Feb	HB805	214	FTR	
4 Mar	HR815	214	FTR	
7 Mar	KJ106	214	FTR	
14 Mar	HB802	214	FTR	
15 Mar	HB803	214	FTR	
21 Mar	HB785	214	FTR	
22 Mar	KJ112	214	FTR	
18 Apr	FK188	59/220/519	Engine failure, DBR	
12 May	SR386	214/1699	Hit trees, COL	Gt. Massingham
22 Jun	FK201	220/1674	U/c collapsed, taxying	Aldergrove
10 Jul	HB765	214	Overshot on landing	Oulton
1946				
8 Jan	FA703	59/206/ 519/521	Ditched, 48N 40W	Atlantic

Appendix IV
CCDU Angle

NON OPERATIONAL EMERGENCIES - CCDU ANGLE

Date	Aircraft	No.	Pilot
1943			
25 Sep	Beaufighter	JL832 (D)	Flt Lt Blackmore

Return to Angle from Northolt
Rear exit opened in flight resulting in an emergency landing at Farnborough

3 Nov	Wellington	MP638 (M)	Flt Lt Blackmore

Pilot's escape hatch opened on takeoff – Airborne for five minutes, emergency landing at base

23 Dec	Halifax	HR672(K)	Flt Lt Houston

Port Inner engine cut on takeoff, returned to base

1944			
13 Feb	Wellington	HF227 (J)	Flt Lt Corrie

Fabric around VP smoldering, returned to base

12 Apr	Wellington	HX202	Fg Off Buck

Electrical system failed; airborne for five minutes; emergency landing

29 May	Wellington	MP516 (M)	Sqn Ldr Holmes DFC & Bar

Leading edge fabric stripped; emergency landing at St Athan

26 Jun	Wellington	HZ409	Flt Lt Houston

Port tyre burst on landing

17 Aug   Wellington   MP516(N)   Flt Lt Silson

Starboard engine failed on take off; airborne for five minutes; emergency landing

8 Oct   Wellington   HF251(A)   Flt Lt Houston

Starboard tyre burst on landing

21 Oct   Liberator   BZ967(F)   Flt Lt Handasyde DFC

Nose wheel tyre burst on landing

14 Dec   Wellington   HF169N   Flt Lt Loweth

Port generator U/S; airborne for 15 minutes

27 Dec   Halifax   HR672(K)   Flt Lt Houston

Airspeed Indicator failed on take off; returned to base

1945

9 Jan   Wellington   MP638(M)   Flt Lt Nixon

Port generator U/S; returned to base

9 Mar   Wellington   HF125(A)   Flt Lt Mervyn-Smith

Pilot declared aircraft U/S; returned to base

28 Jul   Liberator   BZ967(F)   Sqn Ldr Holmes DFC & Bar

Starboard inner engine over revved approaching base; landed safely at Angle

5 Nov   Beaufighter   NE765(K)   Sqn Ldr Holmes DFC & Bar

Starboard tyre burst after landing

8 Dec   Warwick   HF892(L)   Fg Off Edmonds

Fabric stripped; returned to base

9 Dec   Warwick   HF892(L)   Fg Off Edmonds

Undercarriage sluggish; delayed landing

Appendix V

ASWDU
Thorney Island

Date	Aircraft	No.	Pilot
1945			
1 Feb	Wellington	HF206(D)	Fg Off Northrup
Starboard engine failed			
19 April	Wellington	HF206 (D)	Fg Off Cowan
Petrol flaps opened; starboard engine failed; airborne for ten minutes			
3 May	Wellington	NB915 (B)	Flt Lt Urlwyn-Smith DFC
Aircraft struck by lightning; emergency landing			
1946			
3 Jan	Wellington	HF251(A)	Flt Lt Cowan
Radar caught fire; emergency landing			
23 June	Walrus	W3076	Flt Lt Ross
Damaged float landing in sea outside St Mary's Bay, Isles of Scilly; aircraft U/S			

Appendix VI

Authors tour of duty

13 July 1940 to 14 May 1946

Dates	Station	County	Activities
13 Jul 40 – 14 Jul 40	Southampton	Hants	Volunteered at Dorset Street
18 Jul 40 – 27 Jul 40	Cardington	Beds	Reception Centre, Health & IQ tests
27 Jul 40 – 10 Aug 40	Blackpool	Lancs	No.9 Reception Centre; basic training & drill
10 Aug 40 – 30 Sep 40	Cardington	Beds	HQ Staff & airfield defence
30 Sep 40 – 1 Nov 40	Swinderby	Lincs	Signals Section
1 Nov 40 – 14 Feb 41	Blackpool	Lancs	No.10 Reception Centre; Wireless/Morse Training
14 Feb 41 – 24 May 41	Cranwell	Lincs	No.1 Signals School; Advance W/T & Morse training
7 Jun 41 – 5 Jul 41	Benson	Oxon	Signals Section
5 Jul 41 – 26 Jul 41	Penrhos	North Wales	No.9 Bombing & Gunnery School for air gunnery training
29 Jul 41 – 25 Sep 41	Silloth	Cumbria	No.1 Operational Training Unit; Crew flying training
25 Sep 41 – 30 Jun 42	Aldergrove	Co. Antrim	206 Squadron; Operational flying
9 Feb 42 – 10 Feb 42	Stornaway	Scotland	Flying operations, [Det]
29 Apr 42 – 30 Apr 42	Tiree	Scotland	Flying operations, [Det]

23 Jun 42 – 27 Jun 42	Donna Nook	Lincs	Flying operations, [Det]
30 Aug 43 – 30 Aug 42	Benbecula	Scotland	206 Squadron; Operational flying
8 Dec 42 – 14 Dec 42	Burtonwood	Lancs	Technical training, [Det]
3 Sep 42 – 5 Sep 43	Dale	South Wales	CCDU; Research flying
5 Sep 43 – 14 Jan 45	Angle	South Wales	CCDU; Research flying
16 Jan 44 – 22 Jan 44		Gibraltar	Testing GEE Chain
18 Jan 44 – 19 Jan 44	Maison Blache	North Africa	[Det]
22 Jan 44 – 26 Jan 44	Lagens	Azores	[Det]
31 Jan 44 – 8 Feb 44	Long Kesh	NI	Trials with Royal Navy submarine [Det]
14 Jan 45 – 14 May 46	Thorney Island	Hants	ASWDU; Research flying
7 Feb 45 – 24 Feb 45	East Fortune	East Lothian	Trials with HMS *Pollux*, [Det]

Appendix VII

Airfields visited by the author during the Second World War

Date	Station	County
11 Oct 41	Limavady	Co. Londonderry, Northern Ireland
5 Dec 41	Wick	Highland, Scotland
10 Dec 41	Hawarden	Flintshire, North Wales
2 Jan 42	Langford Lodge	Co. Antrim, Northern Ireland
26 Jan 42	Evanton	Highland, Scotland
26 Jan 42	Nutts Corner	Co. Antrim, Northern Ireland
17 May 42	Bircham Newton	Norfolk
17 May 42	Grantham	Lincolnshire
21 May 42	Ballykelly	Co. Londonderry, Northern Ireland
24 May 42	Eglinton	Co. Derry, Northern Ireland
23 Jun 42	North Coates	Lincolnshire
17 Jul 42	Ayr	South Ayrshire, Scotland
5 Sep 42	Prestwick	South Ayrshire, Scotland
1 Mar 43	Skitten	Highland, Scotland
18 Mar 43	Heathfield	South Ayrshire, Scotland
5 May 43	Abbotsinch	Renfrewshire, Scotland
5 May 43	Port Ellen	Argyll & Bute, Scotland
13 Jun 43	Reykjavik	Iceland
23 Jul 43	West Freugh	Dumfries & Galloway, Scotland

7 Aug 43	Speke	Merseyside
8 Aug 43	Snitterfield	Warwickshire
30 Aug 43	Thornaby	Cleveland
10 Sep 43	Davidstow Moor	Cornwall
17 Sep 43	Stormy Down	Brigend, South Wales
22 Sep 43	Harrowbeer	Devon
25 Sep 43	Farnborough	Hampshire
25 Sep 43	Northolt	Greater London
27 Sep 43	Defford	Worcestershire
1 Oct 43	Holmsley South	Hampshire
13 Oct 43	Filton	Avon
14 Oct 43	Colerne	Wiltshire
7 Nov 43	St Mawgan	Cornwall
17 Dec 43	Carew Cheriton	Pembrokeshire, South Wales
17 Dec 43	Haverfordwest	Pembrokeshire, South Wales
18 Dec 43	Talbenny	Pembrokeshire, South Wales
19 Dec 43	Chivenor	Devon
20 Dec 43	Beaulieu	Hampshire
20 Dec 43	Ford	Sussex
20 Dec 43	Gosport	Hampshire
30 Dec 43	Pembroke Dock	Pembrokeshire, South Wales
14 Jan 44	St Eval	Cornwall
11 Feb 44	Llandow	Vale of Glamorgan, South Wales
7 Mar 44	Fairwood Common	Swansea, South Wales
29 Mar 44	St Athan	Vale of Glamorgan, South Wales
24 Apr 44	St Davids	Pembrokeshire, South Wales
24 May 44	Predannack	Cornwall
24 May 44	Weston Zoyland	Somerset
7 Mar 45	Boscombe Down	Wiltshire
22 May 45	Calshot	Hampshire
15 Jun 45	Tarrant Rushton	Dorset
23 Jun 45	St Mary's	Isles of Scilly
25 Jun 45	Portreath	Cornwall
27 Jul 45	Tangmere	Sussex
14 Aug 45	Guernsey	Channel Islands

Aircraft flown in by the author during the Second World War

Make	Type	Home Base	Base 2	Base 3	Flts	Hrs	Mins
Avro	Anson	Thorney Is.	Silloth	Angle	28	22	10
Grumman	Avenger	Thorney Is.			3	1	45
Fairey	Barracuda	Thorney Is.			8	9	55
Fairey	Battle	Penrhos			4	2	35
Bristol	Beaufighter	Angle			16	10	25
Bristol	Blenheim	Penrhos			1	0	55
Consolidated	Catalina	Angle			2	2	15
Fokker	F.XXII	Benbecula			2	1	10
Boeing	Flying Fortress	Benbecula			104	563	20
Handley Page	Halifax	Angle	Thorney Is.		23	33	25
Lockheed	Hudson	Aldergrove	Silloth	Angle	188	418	25
Avro	Lancaster	Thorney Is.			2	1	50
Consolidated	Liberator	Angle	Thorney Is.	45	128	35	
de Havilland	Mosquito	Thorney Is.			1	0	55
Airspeed	Oxford	Silloth			5	7	25
Percival	Proctor	Cranwell	Angle	Thorney Is.	23	15	40
de Havilland	Rapide	Cranwell			2	1	50
Stinson	Reliant	Thorney Is.			1	0	45

Short	Sunderland	Pembroke Dock	Angle		5	14 15
Fairey	Swordfish	Thorney Is.			4	5 30
Vickers	Valentia	Cranwell			2	2 40
Lockheed	Ventura	Long Kesh	Angle		6	17 00
Vickers	Warwick	Thorney Is.	Angle		19	40 25
Supermarine	Walrus	Thorney Is.			5	5 05
Vickers	Wellington	Angle	Thorney Is.		218	347 25
				Total	**717**	**1655 40**

Appendix IX

Ranks held and pay structure

Date of pay	Rank	Style	Daily rate of pay
1940			
13 Jul	Enlisted for duty	-	-
18 Jul	Aircraftsman under training	ACM/UT	2/-d
27 Jul	Aircraftsman 2nd Class	AC2	2/6d
1941			
22 May	Aircraftsman 1st Class	AC1	4/9d
	Wireless Operator	WOP	
7 Jul	Leading Aircraftsman	LAC	6/6d
26 Jul	Sergeant Air Gunner	Sgt	7/9d to 8/-d
		WOP/AG	
1942			
6 Mar	Sergeant Air Gunner Grade II	Sgt	9/-d
		WOP/AG	
1 Aug	Sergeant Air Gunner Grade I	Sgt	10/-d
		WOP/AG	
1 Aug	Flight Sergeant	F/Sgt	10/6d to 12/-d
		WOP/AG	

1943

2 Aug	Warrant Officer	W/O	13/6d
		WOP/AG	
17 Oct	Good Conduct Badge awarded		13/9d
4 Jul*	Pilot Officer	Plt Off	14/6d

*Although the official date of my commissioning was the 4 July 1943 my promotion to Warrant Officer was still proceeded with, similarly, my G.C. badge. In effect I was promoted from A/C U/T through every possible rank up to Flight Lieutenant, other than Corporal.

1944

4 Jan	Flying Officer	Fg Off	18/2d
4 Jul	Flight Lieutenant	Flt Lt	21/9d

Appendix X

Pilots the author flew with, five times or more

Name	Flts	Airfields	Aircraft
Ainsworth, Flt Lt	16	Angle	Beaufighter, Wellington
Blackmore, Flt Lt	25	Angle	Beaufighter, Wellington
Clarke, Fg Off	10	Aldergrove, Benbecula	Hudson, Fortress
Corken, Flt Lt	8	Benbecula, Angle, Thorney Is.	Fortress, Wellington, Proctor, Wellington
Cowen, Flt Lt	31	Thorney Is.	Wellington
Dart, Sqn Ldr	5	Thorney Is.	Barracuda, Liberator, Warwick
Dela Rue, Plt Off	8	Aldergrove	Hudson
Dyer, Flt Sgt	29	Benbecula	Fortress
Edmunds, Fg Off	7	Angle	Warwick
Goodson, Flt Sgt	45	Silloth, Aldergrove	Hudson
Handsasyde DFC, Flt Lt	14	Angle	Liberator, Ventura, Wellington
Hards, Wg Cdr	5	Aldergrove	Hudson
Harrup DSO, Sub Lt	6	Thorney Is.	Barracuda
Hill, Fg Off	5	Aldergrove, Benbecula	Hudson, Fortress

Holmes DFC, Sqn Ldr	11	Angle, Thorney Is.	Anson, Beaufighter, Liberator, Walrus, Warwick, Wellington
Houston, Flt Lt	31	Angle	Halifax, Proctor, Wellington
Ireland, Sgt	10	Aldergrove	Hudson
Johnstone, Sqn Ldr	7	Angle	Halifax
Knibb, Flt Lt	9	Angle	Liberator
Marriot, W/O	62	Silloth, Aldergrove, Benbecula	Hudson, Fortress
Matthew, Sub Lt	7	Thorney Is.	Avenger, Swordfish
Mervyn-Smith, Flt Lt	22	Angle	Hudson, Liberator, Wellington
Morrell, Flt Lt	26	Angle, Thorney Is.	Wellington
Nixon, Sqn Ldr	9	Angle	Catalina, Wellington
Northup, Flt Lt	19	Angle, Thorney Is.	Wellington
Patrick, Sqn Ldr	7	Aldergrove, Benbecula	Hudson
Ross, Flt Lt	11	Angle, Thorney Is.	Anson, Liberator, Proctor, Reliant, Walrus
Silson, Flt Lt	30	Angle, Thorney Is.	Wellington, Warwick
Turner DFC, Flt Lt	5	Thorney Is.	Proctor
Urlwyn-Smith DFC, Flt Lt	6	Thorney Is.	Anson, Wellington
Weir, Plt Off	52	Aldergrove, Benbecula	Hudson, Liberator, Fortress
Wilkinson, Flt Lt	6	Thorney Is.	Liberator, Wellington
Williamson, Plt Off	12	Angle	Anson, Wellington
Wills, Fg Off	5	Aldergrove, Benbecula	Hudson, Fortress
Wyatt, Fg Off	9	Thorney Is.	Anson, Liberator, Warwick, Wellington